India 1885–1947:
The Unmaking of an Empire

SEMINAR STUDIES   IN HISTORY

India 1885–1947:

The Unmaking of an Empire

IAN COPLAND

An imprint of **Pearson Education**

Harlow, England · London · New York · Reading, Massachusetts · San Francisco · Toronto · Don Mills, Ontario · Sydney
Tokyo · Singapore · Hong Kong · Seoul · Taipei · Cape Town · Madrid · Mexico City · Amsterdam · Munich · Paris · Milan

PEARSON EDUCATION LIMITED

Head Office:
Edinburgh Gate
Harlow
Essex CM20 2JE
Tel: +44 (0)1279 623623
Fax +44 (0)1279 431059

London Office:
128 Long Acre
London WC2E 9AN
Tel: +44 (0)20 7447 2000
Fax: +44 (0)20 77240 5771
Website: www.history-minds.com

First published in Great Britain in 2001

© Pearson Education Limited 2001

The right of Ian Copland to be identified as Author
of this Work has been asserted by him in accordance
with the Copyright, Designs and Patents Act 1988.

ISBN 0-582-38173-8

British Library Cataloguing-in-Publication Data
A CIP catalogue record for this book can be obtained from the British Library

10 9 8 7 6 5 4 3 2 1

Typeset by 7 in 10/12 Sabon Roman
Printed in Malaysia, LSP

The Publishers' policy is to use paper manufactured from sustainable forests.

CONTENTS

INTRODUCTION TO THE SERIES

Such is the pace of historical enquiry in the modern world that there is an ever-widening gap between the specialist article or monograph, incorporating the results of current research, and general surveys, which inevitably become out of date. *Seminar Studies in History* is designed to bridge this gap. The series was founded by Patrick Richardson in 1966 and his aim was to cover major themes in British, European and World history. Between 1980 and 1996 Roger Lockyer continued his work, before handing the editorship over to Clive Emsley and Gordon Martel. Clive Emsley is Professor of History at the Open University, while Gordon Martel is Professor of International History at the University of Northern British Columbia, Canada, and Senior Research Fellow at De Montfort University.

All the books are written by experts in their field who are not only familiar with the latest research but have often contributed to it. They are frequently revised, in order to take account of new information and interpretations. They provide a selection of documents to illustrate major themes and provoke discussion, and also a guide to further reading. The aim of *Seminar Studies in History* is to clarify complex issues without over-simplifying them, and to stimulate readers into deepening their knowledge and understanding of major themes and topics.

NOTE ON REFERENCING SYSTEM

Readers should note that numbers in square brackets [5] refer them to the corresponding entry in the Bibliography at the end of the book (specific page numbers are given in italics). A number in square brackets preceded by *Doc.* [*Doc. 5*] refers readers to the corresponding item in the Documents section which follows the main text.

History is replete with 'turning points', markers inserted by historians as a way of organising their narratives of the past. Often, these turning points are suggested by large and dramatic events – events so pregnant with significance that even people living through them were conscious that one era was ending and another beginning. Others, though, which seem important now, from the vantage point of the future, caused barely a ripple at the time they occurred; 1885 in South Asian history is one of them.

By Indian standards, 1885 was not a remarkable year. There were no mutinies, no peasant rebellions, no searing epidemics. Probably the year's biggest event, at least from the viewpoint of the British community, was the conquest of Upper Burma, which so pleased the Queen that she allowed the viceroy of the day, Lord Dufferin, to add the capital of the defeated Burmese king Thibaw, Ava, to his hereditary titles. Yet even that cherished moment of imperial glory did not seem as significant to contemporary eyes as it does to ours, for the British of 1885 did not know, as we do, that this would be the very last major conquest of the Raj, and would effectively complete the expansion of the great Indian Empire. However, while 1885 can genuinely be considered something of a turning point in British imperial affairs, this is not the main reason why many historians have chosen that year to begin, or end, or break, their narratives of modern South Asia. 1885 is considered a significant turning point today primarily because of a meeting which took place in Bombay (Mumbhai) in December, at which a new political organisation was formed: the Indian National Congress. Initially, few grasped the significance of the event. Similar bodies had come into existence – and disappeared – before. However, this one was destined to survive. From humble beginnings, it would go on to spearhead India's fight for independence from British rule; in 1947 it would become the regional ruling power in succession to the British Raj.

In taking 1885 as our starting point we are adopting, therefore, a conventional view of modern South Asian history, one which has the Congress, and the nationalist freedom struggle, as its centrepoint. This is not, these days, a view shared by all scholars. Many left-wing historians, following Marx and Gramsci, believe that far too much attention has been heaped on the mainstream Congress to the exclusion of regional and subaltern elements, and have tried to counterpoint the conventional nationalist accounts with a 'history from below', focusing on the struggles of peasants and workers to achieve, not merely freedom in the political sense, but economic justice at the hands of landlords and capitalists. Again, 1885 does not make much sense as a turning point from the perspective of the economic historians, or of students of Indian religion or art or ecology. Nor, indeed, does it have any meaning for the majority of Pakistani scholars, whose national histories celebrate not the achievement of Congress hegemony but the rejection of it by a substantial portion of the subcontinent's Muslims. The story of modern South Asia has many layers. The narrative of India's march to nationhood is only one strand of a much larger story.

The very complexity of that story, however, puts it beyond the compass of a book of this size. Accordingly, I have settled for a more limited – and manageable – project: to describe and explain the process by which Indians and Pakistanis emancipated themselves from the seemingly iron-clad yoke of British imperialism. This seems to me the aspect of the South Asian story most directly accessible to an international undergraduate audience, and the one most in keeping with the style and purpose of this series. It also goes to the heart of what sets modern India apart from most other countries of Asia, namely its vigorously democratic polity – which in turn begs the question of why India has remained for the most part steadfast in its attachment to parliamentary democracy while Pakistan (and Bangladesh), emergent from the same imperial structure, have repeatedly succumbed to military coups.

AUTHOR'S ACKNOWLEDGEMENTS

In the past forty years, as British government and private archives covering the late colonial period have been opened to the public, the field of modern South Asian history has undergone a quiet but total revolution. The arguments advanced in this book draw heavily on this fine new work. I am also indebted to my colleagues at Monash who offered comments on the manuscript, and to Julie Burbidge who helped assemble and edit the documents. Finally, a word of thanks to my friends at Sunnyrume, who kept the cups of inspiration flowing.

PUBLISHER'S ACKNOWLEDGEMENTS

We are grateful to the following for permission to reproduce copyright material:

Palgrave for extracts from *The Indian Nationalist Movement 1883–1947*, edited by B.N. Pandey (1979), published by Macmillan; and Roli Books Pvt Ltd for an extract from *Partitioned: The Other Face of Freedom*, Volume II, edited by Mushiral Hasan (1995).

In some instances we have been unable to trace the owners of copyright material and we would appreciate any information which would enable us to do so.

LIST OF ABBREVIATIONS

ADC	Aide-de-Camp
AICC	All-India Congress Committee
CPI	Communist Party of India
CWC	Congress Working Committee
GNP	Gross national product
IAS	Indian Administrative Service
ICS	Indian Civil Service
IMS	Indian Medical Service
INA	Indian National Army
INC	Indian National Congress
MLA	Members of the Legislative Assembly
MAO College	Muhammadan Anglo-Oriental College
NWFP	North-West Frontier Province
RSS	Rashtriya Swayamsevak Sangh (Association of National Volunteers)
RTC	Round Table Conference
UP	United Provinces

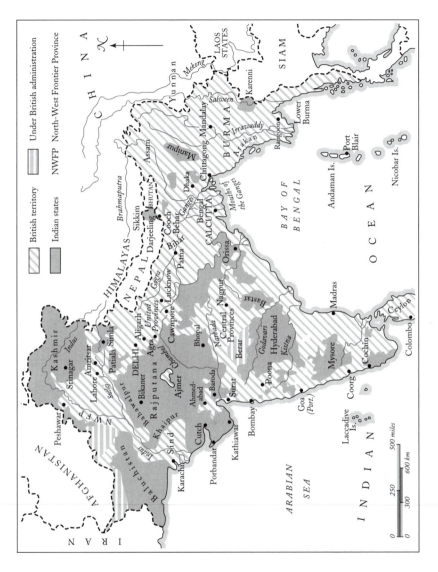

Map 1   The Indian Empire, showing places mentioned in the text

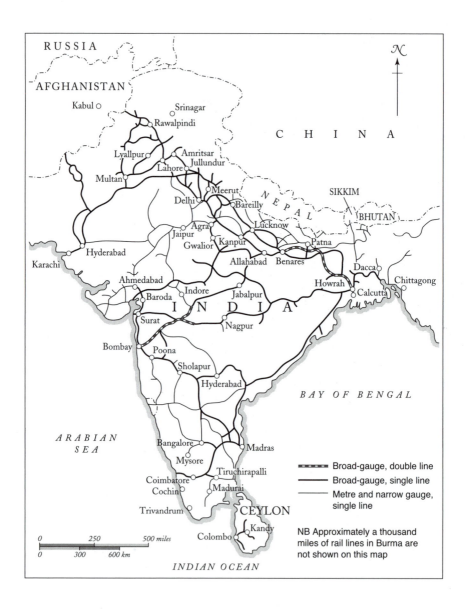

Map 2   The Indian railway network, 1901

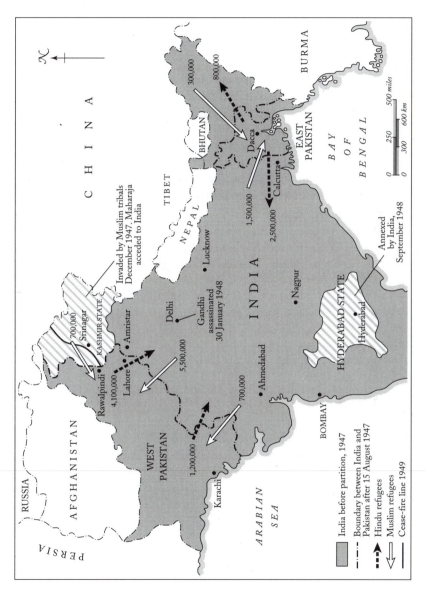

Map 3 The partition of India, 1947

CHRONOLOGY

1885	The Indian National Congress founded at Bombay.
	Upper Burma annexed to the Indian Empire at the end of the Third Anglo-Burmese War.
1892	Indian Councils Act increases Indian participation in local and provincial government.
1897	B.G. Tilak founds the Shivaji Festival as a way of mobilising the masses.
1905	Partition of the province of Bengal under Lord Curzon leads to widespread unrest. Rise of the *Swadeshi* Movement.
1906	Foundation of the All-Indian Muslim League at Dacca.
1907	'Extremists' are expelled from the Indian National Congress after a fracas at Surat.
1909	Morley–Minto reforms increase Indian participation in provincial legislatures. Separate electorates are introduced for Muslims.
1911	King George V annuls the partition of Bengal.
1912	Delhi is made the capital of India.
1914	The Home Rule Movement revives nationalist activities.
	First World War begins.
	The Sultan of Turkey, in his capacity as Khalifa of the Sunni Muslim community, calls for a *jehad* against the Entente Powers.
	Khilafat Movement founded by the Ali brothers.
1915	Gandhi returns to India from South Africa after leading a successful non-violent resistance movement against the Smuts government.
1916	The Lucknow Pact is concluded between the Indian National Congress and the Muslim League to further the cause of Indian self-rule.
1918	First World War ends.
	The Rowlatt Acts threaten civil liberties.
1919	Gandhi calls for a non-violent protest against the Rowlatt Acts. Indians are massacred after protesting at Jallianwala Bagh, Amritsar.

1920	The Communist Party of India is formed.
	The Indian National Congress, led by Gandhi, launches a Non-Cooperation Movement against the government.
1922	Gandhi halts the Non-Cooperation Movement after twenty-two policemen are killed in a violent protest at Chauri Chaura.
	Gandhi is tried and imprisoned.
1924	Gandhi is released from prison suffering poor health.
1927	Establishment of the Simon Commission to study whether India is ready for further constitutional progress. The Indian National Congress boycotts the Commission.
1928	General strikes and protests take place all over India.
	Jawaharlal Nehru and Subhas Chandra Bose emerge as important Congress leaders.
	A resolution for complete independence is passed at the Calcutta session of the Congress in December and civil disobedience is mooted unless India is given 'Dominion Status' within twelve months.
1929	Communist Conspiracy trial at Meerut.
1930	The Civil Disobedience Movement begins with a Gandhi-led march from Ahmedabad to the coast to draw attention to the iniquity of the government's excise on salt. Both Jawaharlal Nehru and Gandhi are arrested in the course of a massive government crack-down.
	The first Round Table Conference, suggested by Lord Irwin, is held in London to discuss Dominion Status for India.
1931	After a pact agreed to in March by Gandhi and Lord Irwin, the British Government releases prisoners, relaxes repressive measures and allows the manufacture of salt in coastal villages in return for the suspension of the Civil Disobedience Movement.
	Gandhi attends the second Round Table Conference in London.
1932	Gandhi is arrested in January. He begins a fast to the death in September to highlight the divisive nature of the Communal Award handed down by British Prime Minister Macdonald as part of the Round Table constitution-making process. Gandhi and Dr Ambedkar (representing the depressed classes) reach an agreement on the representation of the depressed classes in the federal legislature, at which point Gandhi ends his fast.
1934	The Communist Party of India is declared illegal.

1935	A Government of India Act passed in August provides for a federal government in India. It gives a large degree of autonomy to the provinces, although veto power still resides with the viceroy.
1937	The Indian National Congress takes office in six provinces after elections held under the 1935 Act.
1939	Indian nationalist leaders are not consulted before the viceroy involves India in the Second World War. Nationalist leaders counter that they will fight if they are an independent people. Ignored by the viceroy, the elected Congress ministries resign. The Muslim League condemns the viceroy's action but decides to work the constitution.
1940	The Muslim League, at Lahore, demands a separate state of Pakistan.
1941	Subhas Chandra Bose escapes from detention in Calcutta and broadcasts from Berlin, calling for all Indians to revolt. Indian National Congress leaders reject a proposal from the British, delivered by Lord Privy Seal, Sir Stafford Cripps, for Dominion Status at the end of the war.
1942	In August the entire Congress leadership is arrested after calling on the British to 'quit India'. The 'Quit India Movement' begins with widespread rioting and sabotage.
1943	In Tokyo, Subhas Chandra Bose forms a provisional Free Government of India and assumes control of the Indian National Army which has been formed from disaffected Indian POWs in Malaya.
1945	Second World War ends.
1946	A British Cabinet Mission arrives in India to negotiate a transfer of power but disagreements over safeguards for Muslims and the future of Pakistan lead to a stalemate.
	In August, 5,000 people die during communal clashes in Calcutta.
1947	India achieves independence. Jawaharlal Nehru becomes the Prime Minister of India. Muslim League leader Mohammad Ali Jinnah becomes Governor-General of Pakistan. Widespread riots break out across north India. Perhaps 13 million Hindus, Sikhs and Muslims migrate, seeking safety across the new international frontier.

PART ONE THE BACKGROUND

CHAPTER ONE

RULERS AND SUBJECTS

THE POWER OF THE SWORD

The British Raj in India did not come into existence suddenly, fully-fledged; it was built up slowly, often by means of trial and error, over the better part of a hundred years. But by the 1880s, when our story begins, it had achieved what one might call its mature form. Appointment by patronage had largely given way to recruitment by competitive examination; the work of revenue collection had been systematised and to some extent standardised; and a beginning made towards the separation of executive and legislature by the Councils Acts of 1861 and 1892. All the while, the Raj had continued to expand and evolve. By 1887, over 20,000 people were drawing government salaries in excess of rupees 75 a month. Several hundred thousand more held down menial jobs in the postal service, the army, the police, and the public works department. By any standards, the late nineteenth-century Raj was a massive bureaucracy – too massive, some officials complained, for its own good.

Nevertheless it was a government that worked. Far and away the majority of Indians in the late nineteenth century paid their taxes and obeyed the laws. They accepted the Raj as a given in their lives. This, when you think about it, is a remarkable thing: for not only was the Raj, in the last resort, a foreign government, it was racially a government of the very few over the very many. In 1887 there were just over 6,000 Europeans in the public service, about 1,000 in the elite Indian Civil Service (ICS) whose members monopolised the senior administrative posts. In 1921 the entire white population, including women, was only 156,000, which equates to approximately one European for every 1,500 Indians. How did the British maintain control when they were so vastly outnumbered?

The official response to this question (at least down to the 1920s) was usually couched in terms of the 'good government' provided by the Raj. 'Efficiency has been our gospel, the keynote of our administration', boasted Lord Curzon [64 *p. 242*]. This is of course a far from sufficient explanation, but neither should it be dismissed out of hand. Compared to previous Indian governments (at least those of recent memory), the Raj did have a lot to commend it. The ICS, while not quite the platonic cadre of high-minded 'guardians' its apologists have claimed [e.g., 70], was hard-working, conscientious and notably incorrupt. The calibre of some of the other all-India services, such as the Indian Medical Service, was even higher, as the name of Ronald Ross IMS, discoverer of the malaria bacillus, test-ifies. As for the government at large, it was paternalistic, and sometimes despotic, but never arbitrary. Officials worked with textbooks and manuals at their side; the courts operated within the confines of the Civil and Criminal Codes and the Code of Civil Procedure; when not circumscribed by statute, viceregal discretion was shackled by the supervision of the Secretary of State and parliament. Ultimately, this was a rule of law. Moreover, it was a government that could claim to have effected some real improvements. By the turn of the twentieth century some 200 million Indians annually were patronising the British-built railway network (the world's fourth largest); even more were using the government-run postal service. The rail system benefited merchants also as it has been estimated that freight rates on the railways were 80–90 per cent cheaper per ton mile than the charges for bullock-cart carriage. Another success story was irrigation. Canals to divert the seasonal river waters had brought large tracts of wasteland under the plough. Especially (but not only) in the canal colonies, land prices by the end of the century had risen dramatically, which was good news for the small minority of rural-dwellers that actually owned some land. Finally, although the matter is much disputed by historians, there is some evidence in the census and other reports that at least the middle-ranking sections of the population were living better than their forebears [*Doc. 1*]. Amenities widespread by 1900 but unheard of fifty years before included not only the railways but kerosene lamps and piped drinking water. 'Can any other country show anything to compare with this wonderful achievement?', mused former Punjab governor Sir Michael O'Dwyer, after his retirement in 1925 [32 *p. 252*]. The question is moot; but we might concur with O'Dwyer to the extent of hypothesising that people who benefit from a ruling regime are more likely to tolerate its excesses.

Nowdays, however, historians are inclined to put much more emphasis on other factors, in particular the element of power. As noted above, the Indian Empire was defended by a very large, well-equipped, professional standing army. This force could be reinforced, if needed, by regiments of the British regular army. In the early twentieth century, when nationalist agitation began to become a problem, some fifty battalions of the Indian Army, supplemented by artillery, armoured cars and aircraft, were specifi-cally designated to put down insurrection. Supplementing these awesome legions were some 200,000 police officers, some armed with guns, the majority with steel-tipped bamboo staves called *lathi*s, which were capable of breaking open a man's skull at close quarters. Arguably, just the knowledge that this stupendous military might existed, ready to be called out in aid of the civil power if the occasion demanded, was probably enough to keep most of the subject population quiet for most of the time. And that suited the Raj, too. Threat was much cheaper and less complicated than actual coercion [*Doc. 2*]. But when it had to act, the Raj pulled no punches. Rioters who refused police orders to disperse were greeted with *lathi*-charges; 'terrorists' were executed; peddlers of 'sedition' were deported to Burma or the Andaman Islands. The mailed fist was especially evident during wartime, when the government arrogated to itself sweeping additional powers of search, arrest, and detention without trial under the Defence of India Rules. However, the weapon of last resort was the army. It was used infrequently, but when it was called out, the consequences were always terrible. The most infamous of these martial law episodes occurred in April 1919, in the Punjab city of Amritsar, when a peaceful crowd at a political meeting was fired on, without warning, for several minutes by a company of Gurkhas under the command of an ailing and possibly unstable British military officer, Brigadier-General Reginald Dyer. The official body-count was 379 killed and over 1,000 wounded, but was probably, in actuality, much higher. An unrepentant Dyer claimed afterwards that his action had made a 'wide impression' and had considerably undermined the morale of the 'rebel' movement.

But British power in India did not rest simply on force, or the threat of force. Thanks to the work of scholars such as Michel Foucault, we now realise that in addition to the overt instruments of law enforcement, there are other, more subtle agencies of coercion available to the state, such as the mental hospital and the school. In India, as elsewhere, state-sponsored education was used, not just to impart knowledge, but to inculcate obedience to authority. Moreover, that knowledge, itself, was by no means value-neutral. By the latter nineteenth century, British scholarship had generated an impressively vast and ostensibly scientific corpus of historical and sociological data about India. Collectively, this data reflected poorly on Indian society, which was revealed to be hopelessly divided and ridden with outmoded superstitions. Conversely, it showed up the 'modern' West in a very positive light [47; 55]. Together these two understandings comprised a persuasive explanation – and justification – for British rule. Caught up in the paradigm, Indians became unknowingly complicit in their own subjection.

More controversial is the human variable in the colonial equation. As we have seen, the British in India numbered scarcely 200,000, and of these only a fraction actually ruled, in the sense of administered; at the policy and command level, the Raj was run by about 1,000 members of the ICS. Thus it was said that the ICS constituted the 'steel frame' of British rule in India. Explicit in this steel frame argument is the Kiplingesque notion that the average British district officer was a pretty capable chap who worked hard, lived clean, and had little regard for personal danger. Implicit is the suggestion that the district officers exercised a kind of sway over the ordinary people they ruled, a sway that was partly rooted in deference for their position as the representatives of the government, the *sarkar*, but was also a function of the sharp physical and social differences that set them apart from their subjects: differences of height, colour, dress and demeanour, that in status-conscious India marked them out as men of high caste, 'twice-born' as the local saying went. Today, in the light of modern research, the argument looks a trifle overblown. Recent work on recruitment to the ICS has shown that it never became the first career-choice for the British public school and university elite, as people like Jowett of Balliol had hoped. While the tough examinations excluded downright mediocrities, they let in lots of people who were intellectually fairly average and gifted with no great athleticism either: hardly supermen material [63]. Yet these unlikely lads performed, sometimes heroically. Leonard Woolf once recalled of his time in Ceylon (Sri Lanka), that the English colonials there appeared to have modelled themselves on Rudyard Kipling's fictional characters. The same role-playing seems to have happened in India. Coming as they often did from service families, the men of the ICS were exposed from an early age to tales of imperial valour. Their training reinforced this ethic, as did the propaganda then circulating about white racial superiority, and contact with their peers on arrival in India. Gradually the young recruits assimilated the authority roles expected of them, and with each passing year the deference they received made it easier for them to believe that Indians actually wanted to be ruled. 'I had the illusion, wherever I was, that I was infallible and invulnerable in my dealings with Indians', recalls Sir Walter Lawrence in his memoirs [71 *p. 54*] [*Doc. 3*]. What made the district officers generally successful as people-managers was their inordinate self-belief. As Lawrence confesses, it was a self-belief founded in large part on illusion. But the illusion was good enough to fool a lot of people for quite a long time.

Force and personal suasion together go a long way to explaining how the British kept control of the subcontinent until 1947. Yet was military power enough? Was personal influence enough, given that the district officers had on average 100,000 people to look after and could not be everywhere at once? At one level the answer is obvious: consider what would have happened if, in the early twentieth century, the entire population of 300 millions had risen up as one against their foreign rulers? Or even a substantial fraction of that number, say fifty millions? Surely not even the might of the Indian Army could have withstood such a massive movement? Alternatively, could the Raj have survived if all its native soldiers had deserted, or if its contractors had stopped supplying it with goods, or if a substantial section of the peasantry had refused to pay the land tax? Again, the answer is probably 'no'. But neither of these frightening eventualities was ever on the cards. Revolts do not occur spontaneously; they are planned and led. Even if the people of India had been of one mind and purpose, mobilising such a vast multitude would have been a logistical nightmare. But they were not. As history would show, and as the high priests of colonial knowledge had long insisted, the Indian population was far too socially heterogeneous ever to suffer itself to be welded into a single subcontinental commonality.

As for the alternative, selective civil disobedience, the problem there, as Mahatma Gandhi would discover in 1920, was fear. People who thwarted the government were punished – beaten, jailed, fined. Many Indians wanted to stand up to the Raj; few were prepared to face the dire consequences of law-breaking.

However, the British needed more from the Indian population than mere passivity; they needed cooperation. They needed soldiers for their army, clerks for their offices, lawyers for their courts, guests for their receptions. Beyond that, they needed stalwart friends out in the community, influential intermediaries who could help them sell their message of improvement to the masses. They got them. It is in this sense that some historians suggest that British rule in India rested substantially on the consent of the governed.

COLLABORATION

Why did some Indians offer their services to the Raj? Why (to use more loaded language) did they collaborate? There were both negative and positive reasons. The negative reasons had to do with the way government service was perceived, or rather, how it was *not* perceived, within the subject community. Until quite late in the piece, most Indians who thought about such matters saw nothing very strange in the fact that India was part of an empire. Much of the civilised world, in the nineteenth century, was made up of polyglot empires, and India itself had an extensive imperial tradition. Nor was the racial aspect all that disconcerting; the previous kings of Delhi had been Mughals from Central Asia. Service with the Raj was not, therefore, in most eyes, unpatriotic. As for the positive reasons, there were many: habit and custom; admiration for British culture; simply the desire for a decent job. But the common factor in all collaborative decisions was an expectation of reward – a salary, a favour, an honour, a raise in status. Meeting these expectations, anticipating them, became a major preoccupation of the Indian authorities during the latter nineteenth century.

The original strategy had been to cultivate the urban professional classes, whose skills were essential to the business of administration. Initially, this had proved quite easy. Groups like the Bengali *bhadralok* ('respectable folk') and the Parsis of Bombay had flocked to the Raj's standard, drawn not simply by the financial and status rewards of public service employment, but by the heady allure of Western thought and culture. By the 1830s, elite competition for jobs and 'English' education was so great that senior members of government like T.B. Macaulay became convinced that it was only a matter of time before there emerged, in India, 'a class of persons Indian in blood and colour, but English in taste, in opinions, in morals and in intellect' [10 *p. 601*]. However, by the 1870s the high hopes held out for this hegemonic project had begun to crumble. While there were still plenty of candidates for government jobs, their character disappointed. Their Englishness seemed quaint and superficial, their undoubted cleverness flashy and bookish, and they showed a disconcerting lack of interest in manly sports. What was more, the middle class exhibited signs of losing its once-uncritical infatuation with British rule. As late as 1877 one of the leading figures of Calcutta society, Keshub Chandra Sen, could still unblushingly refer to Queen Victoria as 'an instrument in the hands of Providence to elevate this degraded country in the scale of nations' [10 *p. 619*]. But even as Keshub was being warmly applauded by his *bhadralok* audience, other Bengalis were striking a more discordant note. Especially in the vernacular press, British benevolence was being called into question. Was British rule designed for India's benefit, or Britain's? While none of these critics went so far as to call for British withdrawal, their negativism rankled. Officials started to talk of the 'disloyalty' of the *babu* class. No longer convinced that the masses could be bought merely by the provision of good government [*Doc. 4*], increasingly disenchanted with the abilities and attitudes of the Western-educated, the government moved to cement its ties with other, potentially less troublesome, sections of society.

Initially, its gaze fell on the princes and the aristocracy. The princes, some 600 in number, had been saved from oblivion by the Queen's proclamation of 1858 pledging no more annexations, and given a new dynastic lease of life by Lord Canning's *sanads* of 1862, which allowed them to adopt heirs without restriction. Now the British strove to bring them into the political mainstream: the rulers were made the centrepiece of Lord Lytton's 'imperial assemblage' of 1877 and Curzon's Delhi Durbar of 1903; they were invited to royal occasions in England; the more efficient princely armies were utilised to help defend the frontier. In a much publicised initiative, the government in 1908 solicited the princes' advice on how to deal with sedition, and when war came the Nizam of Hyderabad was encouraged to speak out against the Sultan of Turkey's *fatwa* calling on Muslims to fight with the Central Powers in the name of Islam. In 1917 the Maharaja of Bikaner was appointed to the Imperial War Cabinet, and in 1921 the rulers were assigned a formal constitutional role with the creation of the Chamber of Princes at Delhi. The princes welcomed these initiatives, and responded enthusiastically, in part because it was made plain to them by Lord Minto in 1909 that if they played their parts properly, they could count on being left alone to rule their own states more or less as they liked. As for the British, they reckoned they had made a pretty good bargain. First, maintaining the princely states relieved them of direct responsibility for a large part of the subcontinent (about one-third). This had important cost-saving implications. Secondly, the princely alliance connected British rule, however tenuously, with Indian tradition. The system of dynastic governance was deeply rooted in the Hindu past. The princes themselves were considered by many to carry the blood-lines of the ancient Hindu god-kings. Having these charismatic rulers as allies gave the Raj a much needed touch of legitimacy [40].

The 'aristocracy' was the official term for the titled and landed folk of British India. Unlike the princes, the aristocracy paid taxes and were subject to Indian law. Yet they, too, were influential people. Often, like the maharajas, of *kshatriya* (warrior) caste, they commanded deference by virtue of their high status. And as large landlords, they exercised a powerful economic sway over the local peasantry. Intuitively, the British had always known this. After all, they too hailed from a society dominated by rural magnates. But their respect for the social power of the aristocracy increased exponentially in 1857, when disaffected rural elements such as the *talukdars* of Oudh (Awadh) rose up in revolt across large tracts of the Gangetic plain, carrying their occupancy-tenants with them. As the rebellion dragged on into its second year, the government abandoned its ideologically-driven plan to dispossess the landlords and redistribute their land to the peasants, and began to conciliate them. The *talukdars* and *zamindars* (landlords) were confirmed in their holdings, which were made subject to primogeniture to prevent them fragmenting. In 1861 they were organised into the British Indian Association of Oudh. Over the following decades they were given economic assistance and special access to officials, were inducted as magistrates and justices of the peace, and were nominated to legislative councils [55; 58].

Last but not least, the Raj struck up a fruitful relationship with a section of its Muslim subjects, notably that segment of the north Indian Muslim elite which belonged to the circle of Sir Saiyyid Ahmad Khan at Aligarh. As we shall see, this would become, in time, probably the most important strategic alliance of all; certainly it would prove the most consequential. However, at the time the *rapprochement* was unexpected. British rule had not done the Muslims many favours. The English East Indian Company's conquests had snuffed out most of the Muslim ruling dynasties, and its policy of resuming tax-free lands had cut deeply into the pockets of the Muslim gentry. The Crown's push after 1858 towards the replacement of Urdu or Persian as the language of record in government offices by English, which relatively few Muslims then knew well, had accelerated the process of economic decline. (In 1886, 1,230 Hindus passed the entrance examination for the University of Calcutta, but only 91 Muslims.) Most elite Indian Muslims by the latter nineteenth century felt lost and confused; a few sought an outlet for their angst in violence, as when, in 1871, a Wahabi zealot murdered the viceroy Lord Mayo, an act that reinforced the prevailing British official picture of Muslims as a 'race' given to fanaticism.

More than anyone else it was Sir Saiyyid who turned this unpromising situation around. Having broken ranks with his proud, orthodox-leaning family, and taken service with the British, he rose quickly in the ranks of the North-West Provinces administration to the post of deputy magistrate of Bijnor. There, he helped save the treasury from falling into rebel hands in 1857, an act of gallantry (or perhaps prescience) that earned him a knighthood and a lucrative pension from his grateful superiors. His own career, therefore, provided a fine advertisement for the benefits of collaboration. Yet Sir Saiyyid's attraction to the British went well beyond considerations of patronage. He admired the integrity of the British officials with whom he came into contact. Especially after a visit to England in 1870, he became convinced that British rule was an essential prerequisite to the regeneration of India, and that his community had been tragically misguided, hitherto, in turning its back on Westernisation. Accordingly, he spent his retirement years trying to build bridges between the government and the Muslim elite. He wrote a number of tracts demonstrating that modern scientific thought was not repugnant to the *Qur'an*. He set up a school in his home town of Aligarh, the Muhammadan Anglo-Oriental (MAO) College, where Muslim boys from good families could go to partake of the new education. He established a Scientific Society where the latest Western discoveries could be discussed. In 1886 he founded the Muhammadan Educational Congress, and in 1888 the United Patriotic Association to spread the gospel of loyalty to the Raj.

Meanwhile, on the British side, officials such as Sir William Wilson Hunter were pressing the view that the Muslims were a 'backward' community deserving of the government's compassion and support. Thus by the time the MAO College opened its doors in 1875 the basis had been laid for a partnership. And in the short term at least, it proved a very rewarding one for both parties. The Aligarh College itself profited handsomely from government subventions and from a bending of the grant-in-aid rules. More generally, the Muslim professional elite benefited from Lord Dufferin's order that local governments should henceforward bear in mind 'the depression of a numerous and influential class' in deciding the 'distribution of places of emolument' [43 *pp. 158–9*]. After 1900, as we shall see, Muslim political claims too were facilitated by the privileged official access afforded to community leaders. For their part, the British secured another set of useful friends.

However, if the British profited from the collaboration of influential sections of Indian society, they also gained from the increased competition between rival castes and communities that collaboration provoked. The more some groups positioned themselves in the orbit of the Raj, the more others, in reaction, took themselves further away. Of course, the divisions within Indian society which underlay this jockeying for position had always been there. But they were enhanced by the new opportunities and challenges thrown up by the modernising impact of the Raj [61]. And as time went by, the British realised they could, to some extent, manipulate the process by extending or withholding their favours, or by taking administrative decisions that advantaged one group over another. Curzon's 1904 decision to create a new, dominantly Muslim, province of East Bengal was one such. This has been described, rightly, as an imperial strategy of 'divide and rule'; but as the Muslim leader Muhammad Ali observed wryly at the London Round Table Conference of 1930, 'there is a division of labour here. *We* divide and *you* rule' [41 *p. 36*].

THE LIMITED RAJ

Folklore paints the Indian Empire as a kind of super-state, huge, immovable, majestic and omnipotent. Until recently, that has also been the view of the historical profession. Although they tended to disagree violently about the intentions and impact of colonialism in the subcontinent, down to the 1970s both British and Indian writers had no doubts about the absoluteness of British governmental power. But was the Raj, in actuality, the formidable machine it appears to be? Even assuming that the goal of British rule was despotism, was the Raj capable of imposing one?

As we have seen, the British had access to a vast and outwardly impressive reservoir of military and police power. However, while the army was quite capable of defeating any organised insurgency, it was too heavy and blunt an instrument to be of much use as a means of crowd control, a point acknowledged by Lord Ripon in 1881: 'I hold as strongly as any man that we must be careful to maintain our military strength; but, whatever may have been the case in the past, we cannot now rely on military power alone' [38 *p. 100*]. Accordingly, it was left to the police to hold the line from day to day. Yet they were stretched too thinly to maintain more than a token presence outside the big towns. In Madras the ratio of policemen to population around 1900 was 1:2000; in Bengal it was even lower. Although much was made of the 'British peace' in India, this was true only in the limited sense that the subcontinent under British rule was spared the devastation of major interstatal wars; civil violence (murders, robberies, riots) remained endemic. Likewise, a lack of reliable resources handicapped the efforts of the civilian bureaucracy headed by the ICS. With only a few hundred British personnel available for district administration, most of the adminstrative work at the local (sub-district and village) level had to be left to Indian subordinates who were comparatively poorly paid, drawn from a narrow range of castes, and often closely connected with the dominant elites in the district. Many of these subordinate officials, recent research has shown, were quite venal and corrupt. They took bribes, jobbed their relatives into office, and conspired with local landowners to defraud the government by falsifying records. In one instance, in Tanjore District in 1884, over 800,000 rupees that should have gone into consolidated revenue ended up in the pockets of a clique of Madrasi Brahmins led by the collector's chief native assistant [66]. At the grass-roots level, British authority was gravely compromised in its dependance on the advice, mediation and agency of local men driven by agendas quite different from those of their superiors.

Much, then, depended on the compliance the British could purchase from their subjects by way of deals and favours. But while collaborators were not hard to find, the government in some cases was unsure about the value of their support. 'Whether the aristocracy themselves are very powerful may be doubted', opined Lord Salisbury, 'and any popularity we may achieve with them is not much to lean upon in a moment of trial' [61 *p. 193*]. This bleak assessment was fully born out when the National Agriculturalist Party, composed mainly of *talukdars*, was routed by nationalists at the 1923 provincial elections. And similar concerns were held about the princes. During the latter nineteenth century the Raj was compelled to intervene repeatedly in the states to repair social infrastructure damaged by gross misrule; in some cases the responsible rulers had to be deposed as a preliminary to reform. These crises of rulership did little to enhance the reputations either of the princely order or of their feudal overlords.

Older studies of British rule in India were premised on the assumption that the things the British said they intended to do, actually happened. The truth is otherwise. Unable to rule simply by main force, reliant on legions of subordinates of doubtful loyalty to keep the wheels of administration turning, ultimately dependant upon the tacit or active cooperation of significant sections of Indian society, the British might dream of moulding the subcontinent and its people in their image, but the governmental machinery at their disposal was never adequate for such a herculean task. Moreover, the nature of the imperial compact mitigated against radical change. At the macro-level, the British found their freedom of action with regard to India and its people increasingly curtailed by the need to appease their influential supporters. The landlords, the princes, the elite Muslims were wealthy, generally orthodox groups with a vested interest in the perpetuation of the *status quo*. Acknowledging this, the Raj after the Mutiny put the brakes on radical social reform. Similarly, at the micro-level, administrative innovation was frustrated by the undertakings entered into by venal subordinate officials with their shadowy paymasters, and by the peasantry's inbred (and to some extent justified) suspicion of the motives of prying government servants [*Doc. 5*].

The British were the masters of India; but they were also its servants, bonded to the subcontinent by the iron discipline of duty. They were in a sense the captives of the people they ruled. Before he became a famous English novelist, George Orwell served for some years in Burma as a member of the Indian Police, and many graphic memories from this formative period infuse his writings. One of them concerns a time when he was called upon to shoot a rogue elephant that was destroying the crops of a village. He did not want to shoot the beast; at the last he wanted nothing more than to walk away. But inertia, fear of ridicule, and something that might just have been the call of duty held him fast. Slowly, mechanically, he raised his rifle and took aim. 'I perceived in this moment', he wrote later, 'that when the white man turns tyrant it is his own freedom that he destroys' [35 *p. 239*].

PART TWO ANALYSIS

CHAPTER TWO

IMPERIAL DILEMMAS

THE ILLUSION OF PERMANENCE

The mid-nineteenth century had been a testing time for the British Raj in India. The two Sikh wars of the 1840s, which paved the way for the annexation of the Punjab in 1849, had been costly victories. In 1857 a loose coalition of mutinous *sepoys* (native soldiers), rural magnates, dispossessed rulers and Muslim religious leaders had briefly threatened the tenure of the Raj in north India. Throughout the 1860s and 1870s, the imperial peace was disturbed by a series of peasant insurrections in Bengal, Bihar, Punjab and the Bombay Deccan. But by the mid-1880s the dust was starting to settle. Although the terrible memory of 1857 still haunted the British community, planters' wives in lonely stations no longer waited in dread for a recurrence. There had been no further mutinies. Nor was there, as yet, any indication of widespread dissent among the civilian population of the cities. The professional classes still jockeyed for places in the public service; businessmen still competed for government contracts; intellectuals still took nourishment from the corpus of Western learning. As for politics, the few avowedly political organisations then in existence were all thoroughly gentlemanly bodies – gentlemanly in the sense both of gender and style. They met only occasionally, and their criticisms of government policy were respectful and polite; they had no agenda of agitation. Even the strongest of them, the Indian National Congress, seemed to the government so feeble and moribund that Curzon could condescendingly (but in all seriousness) announce in 1900 that his ambition was to 'assist it to a peaceful demise' [19 *p. 150*] [*Doc. 6*].

Besides, for every Congressman who carped about the hardships imposed by British rule, there were a dozen Indians who proclaimed just as publicly that British rule had been the making of India. We have already noted Keshub Chandra Sen's royal eulogy of 1877. Equally striking is the sentiment expressed in the celebrated novel *Anandamath*, by Keshub's contemporary Bankim Chandra Chatterjee, which ends with its guerilla hero giving up his career of armed struggle in the belief that the common people would be happier under British dominion. But the British did not need public tributes from the famous to know that the vast majority of the townsfolk were steadfastly loyal. They saw evidence of it at every turn, not least in the behaviour of their servants. Virtually every Anglo-Indian memoir has its tale of native servants going out on a limb for their white masters and mistresses. And the same trope crops up regularly in contemporary English fiction: as, for example, in Flora Annie Steel's story of a native 'bearer' who secretly offers sacrifices to the goddess Kali in a futile effort to save the life of the young sahib in his charge. From a modern viewpoint this behaviour reeks more of sycophancy than of real loyalty; but that is not how it was seen at the time.

If the British rulers of India were worried about anything in the 1880s, it was the disposition of the peasantry, the 'silent' rural masses who comprised the overwhelming majority of their subjects. But the countryside was no longer the cauldron of unrest it had been in 1857. Capitalist production for the market was taking hold, and in its wake, a new class of rich peasants was emerging – farmers who owned their land, employed hired labour to work it, and marketed the surplus produce. In the 1860s these peasants had sown cotton. Cotton was then fetching windfall prices owing to the Union blockade of the Confederate South, which had caused American supplies of the crop to virtually dry up. Afterwards they had turned to jute and groundnuts, but particularly wheat. By the 1880s, officials were excitedly forecasting a 'wheat boom' in the Narbada valley of central India; and similar up-beat reports were coming in from the Punjab and Gujarat. Peasants with land and crops to sell were suddenly starting to make big money, and signs of new wealth were everywhere to be seen. 'They have [now] almost without exeption good *pucca* [proper] houses, built with an elaborate main entrance (*darwaza*) which is easily distinguishable from the houses of the tenants', marvelled the Collector of Hoshangabad District in the Central Provinces [65 *p. 275*]. Meanwhile, the situation of those further down the rural hierarchy was ameliorated by the establishment of credit cooperatives and by the passage, between 1859 and 1885, of a series of acts giving legal security of tenure to farmers who could prove twelve years' continous occupancy of the same plot. To be sure, the level of rural prosperity varied widely between classes and regions. Periodically, even during 'boom' years, large areas and millions of lives were devastated by famine. The most serious of these outbreaks, during 1899–1900, affected 60 millions and caused at least five millions to die prematurely from malnutrition and disease. Nor would the 'golden age' of the rich peasant last much beyond the turn of the century. Fortuitously for the British, however, the plight of the rural underclass did not, at least in the late nineteenth century, translate into anger against the government. Blinkered by illiteracy and parochialism, the peasantry was unable to make the causal connection, that now seems so obvious to economic historians, between the growing shortage of grains for domestic consumption and the free-market policies of the administration. Victims blamed nature, or their landlords. The rural masses may not have been, as the British surmised, contented, but for a quarter of a century they remained quiescent. From the Raj's perspective, that was the key thing. When in 1907 the dam finally did break, with an outbreak of riots over irrigation fees in the Punjab canal colonies, the shock of the event was all the greater for being wholly unexpected.

As recipients of a classical education, the British ruling class knew all about the decline of Greece and the fall of Rome. But they failed to apply the obvious analogy to their own imperial follies. They thought the British Empire was different, better. They believed it would prove more durable. The empire in India, especially, seemed to them to be strong enough to last forever. Many, perhaps most, Britons presumed that it would. Writing to the secretary of state in 1912, the viceroy Lord Hardinge opined: 'there can be no question as to the permanency of British rule in India' [38 *p. 197*]. Even as late as 1923, by which time the situation had changed dramatically, the government's planning included an assumption that the Indian Army would continue to be largely British-officered until well into the 1950s. The mindset reflected here is one that goes beyond mere arrogance. It is one of total self-assurance, a self-assurance grounded not just in an unshakeable conviction that the Raj could survive any challenge, but in the belief that it was the racial destiny of white men to rule the world [46].

Moreover, quite apart from any larger considerations of race and duty, the British felt compelled to stay in India to honour the various commitments they had made there. Specifically, they had commitments to their political allies, the princes and the landed aristocracy. Not only were these groups ultimately reliant for their continued privileged existence upon British military and financial support, but in the case of the princes at least the British had clear contractual obligations, enshrined in solemn treaties, to supply military assistance if such was required to keep them on their thrones. The 1802 treaty with Hyderabad actually stipulated how many British battalions and pieces of artillery the nizam had the right to call upon in times of need. These legal ties would seriously complicate Britain's exit from India in the 1940s. More generally, the British felt a moral, but no less binding, obligation to the 'minorities', such as the Muslims, and to the vulnerable, voiceless multitudes in the villages. As a parliamentary report put it: 'There must be an authority in India, armed with adequate powers, able to hold the scales evenly between conflicting interests and to protect those who have neither the influence nor the ability to protect themselves' [2 *p. 14*]. Finally, and more abstractly, they felt they owed it to the Indian people to try to complete their *mission civilisatrice*. Although much had been achieved, there still remained much to be done by way of implanting modern institutions and equipping the subcontinent with an efficient infrastructure, and the officials of the 1880s and 1890s had little faith in the ability or inclination of Indians to carry on the good work of improvement if they were to leave. To glazed Victorian eyes, the Indian elites consisted of either warriors (the 'martial races') or pen-pushers. The former, such as the Rajputs, the Jat-Sikhs and the Pathans, were considered virile but slow-witted; the latter, such as the Kayasthas and Vaidyas of Bengal, and the Chitpavan Brahmins of Maharashtra, were categorised as sly, cowardly and effeminate, 'moral if not physical degenerates' [26 *p. 59*] [*Doc. 7*]. Neither class seemed to the British to possess the ingredients required to run a country: 'If our Government were to cease', wrote long-time Indian Finance Member Sir John Strachey, 'the miseries from which [the subcontinent] ... has been rescued would inevitably and instantly return' [33 *pp. 212–13*].

All this, however, begs an obvious question. If the British in the late nineteenth century were so wedded to the task of administering India, and had the means, as they maintained, to neutralise any internal or external threat to their position there, why, just fifty years later, did they grant the country its freedom?

BENEFITS AND COSTS

The beginnings of an answer to that question can be hazarded with reference to the changing nature of the economic–strategic nexus between Britain and India between the 1880s and the 1940s. For all the rhetoric about a civilising mission, altruism was never at the forefront of the imperial project; empires are acquired primarily for reasons of self-interest, and to serve metropolitan ends. It follows, therefore, that the maintenance of the Indian Empire was always conditional on it continuing to provide Britain with money, power and influence. Between the wars, its usefulness to Britain significantly declined. Moreover, empires do not come free. There was the matter of costs to be considered: the expenditure of elite manpower, overheads, political effort. So long as the subcontinent remained a hot property, London was prepared to invest heavily to keep it; once its value declined, the outlay in British lives became increasingly unsustainable.

Such is the broad argument. Let me now flesh it out by reviewing the benefits to Britain of dominion in India, itemising its costs and tracing the changing balance of the equation between 1914 and 1939.

During the nineteenth century, India became the single largest overseas market for British manufactures. There were several reasons. One was the happy coincidence that Britain's biggest industrial export, cotton textiles, was a product in high demand in the bazaars of the subcontinent. Another was the opening in 1869 of the Suez Canal, which drastically reduced travelling time and thus freight costs between Europe and Asia. But the main one was the government's control over tariff policy. At a time when other developing countries such as Australia and the United States were imposing protective duties on foreign imports as a way of encouraging domestic industries, India reduced its tariff, in 1882, from 3½ per cent *ad valorum* to zero. Later, when it was put back as a revenue-raising measure, the government obliged Lancashire by clapping a countervailing excise on local manufactures. Not surprisingly, though, this cosy imperial relationship was anathema to Indian nationalists; and when the government in the early twentieth century found itself (for reasons we shall explain in Chapter 3) in the position of having to conciliate the nationalist movement, tariff control was one of the things it felt obliged to concede. In 1918 London agreed that the government of India could impose a tariff; in 1923 a tariff board was established in Delhi which two years later abolished the hated domestic excise; by 1931 India had a substantial protective tariff. Meanwhile, the increasing diversification of British industry, and the rise of home-grown demand in Britain itself, especially in the area of the newer industrial products (such as cars and electrical goods), made the subcontinental market less vital to the country's economic health. In combination, these factors resulted in a drop in the British share of Indian imports between 1913 and 1938 of 62 per cent in the case of cotton piece goods, 35 per cent in the case of general machinery and 18 per cent in the case of chemicals. By the 1940s the possession of India was no longer vital to the continued prosperity of British industry [79].

It was a similar story with the Indian Army. In the 1880s British prime minister Lord Salisbury accurately described the Indian Army as 'an English barrack in the oriental seas from which we may draw any number of troops without paying for them' [79 *p. 341*]. If anything, India's contribution to imperial defence in the early twentieth century was even greater. Between 1914 and 1918, it provided (and paid for, at a cost to Indian revenues of some £146 million) nearly 1.5 million troops and non-combatants and over 180,000 pack animals for the French and Middle Eastern fronts. By the early 1920s, over 70 battalions of Indian troops were on imperial guard duty in Egypt, Iraq, Palestine and sundry other trouble-spots. Again, however, the Indian government found itself hard-pressed to justify to the Indian public an arrangement so prejudicial to Indian finances. Faced in mid-1920 with demands from London for an additional contribution of troops to Iraq, the government of India dug their heels in, and the secretary of state was compelled to concede the political force of their objection. 'So far as India is concerned', he reluctantly concluded, 'all idea of initiating as a normal peace measure such a scheme, whereby she is to become the base for vast military operations in the Middle East and the Far East, must be definitely abandoned; [even] if public opinion in India would tolerate it, Indian revenues cannot bear the charge' [79 *p. 360*]. By 1923 an understanding had been reached between London and Delhi that the Indian Army should no longer in the ordinary course of events be extensively deployed overseas on garrison duty, and that any future commitments of that nature should be paid for by the British government. In 1938 this convention was firmed up with the signature of an agreement limiting India's financial liability in wartime to campaigns undertaken exclusively for the forward defence of the subcontinent.

Yet if some aspects of the Indo-British relationship underwent something of a sea-change between the wars, others, such as the intergovernmental monetary transfers from India to Britain to pay for the upkeep of the India Office and the pensions of retired ICS officers (the payments referred to euphemistically as Home Charges) remained fairly constant. Significantly, the Home Charges, along with debt repayments, were among the budgetary items excluded under the 1935 Government of India Act from the purview of the Indian legislature. Nor was the Indian Empire in the late 1930s any less prestigious than it had been fifty years earlier. Therefore, while the imperial position in South Asia in 1939 was definitely not what it had been fifty years earlier, neither had it slipped so far as to make the British think of imminent withdrawal. As late as 1942 Winston Churchill made it clear that he had 'not become the King's First Minister in order to preside over the liquidation of the British Empire' [42 *p. 162*]. To understand why, at the end, the imperial will to rule in respect of India collapsed so suddenly, we need to consider other factors. This brings us, initially, to the question of costs.

Despite having access to an impressive armoury of new technologies – motor cars, aeroplanes, radio, the telephone, medicine for malaria – twentieth-century administrators found India a more difficult place to administer than their late nineteenth-century predecessors had done. In the 1880s, the number of Indians who thought about political issues was rather small; nor, as we noted earlier, were they well-organised. These Westernised critics represented no threat to the government's position. Twenty years later, it was a very different scene. The national movement was much bigger and more resolute. It no longer petitioned; it made demands. What is more, it showed itself increasingly ready to back its criticisms of the government with agitation – marches, demonstrations, boycotts (especially, after 1905, of foreign cloth) and acts of intimidation. There were even isolated attacks on officials. In 1897 the Plague Commissioner of Bombay and his aide-de-camp were murdered in Poona by an angst-ridden Chitpavan Brahmin named Damodar Chapekar; B.C. Allen, the district magistrate of Dacca, was killed in 1907; the following year a bomb intended for Bengal's chief presidency magistrate took the lives of two English ladies travelling on a train; in 1909 assassins' bullets cut down the collector of Nasik and Sir William Curzon-Wylie, ADC to the secretary of state (on a London street); in 1913 the viceroy, Lord Hardinge, narrowly escaped death when a bomb struck the *howdah* of his elephant during a parade in Delhi. Although the terrorists managed between 1897 and 1947 to kill or injure only a tiny fraction of the British and Indian administrative elite, and although the government as a matter of principle refused to be intimidated by these actions, they did exact, over time, a psychological toll – as did, indeed, the business of repressing the upswell of dissent which became, of necessity, more and more a routine feature of Indian administration.

Every large organisation has its sprinkling of pathological types, and there is no reason to think that the British Raj was any different. General Dyer, the 'hero' of Amritsar, was perhaps one of those. Certainly his testimony to the subsequent inquiry suggests a mind warped by paranoia [*Doc. 8*]. However Dyer and his ilk were untypical. The vast majority of the ICS were basically decent men with normal instincts: men who did not relish committing violence personally or, for that matter, giving the orders that set it in motion. As officially-sanctioned violence became more and more commonplace, more and more an integral part of the process of ruling India, the job itself grew progressively and inexorably more stressful. We know this from, among other things, the number of ICS officers who took advantage of new rules introduced in 1922 to take early retirement or transfer to the Colonial Service, which looked after territories where the natives were thought to be more passive and obedient. Twenty-two resigned in 1923 and twenty-one in 1924.

Moreover, the growing tumult in India seems to have discouraged many potential future administrators from applying for the Service. Between 1904 and 1913, some 500 Englishmen were appointed to the ICS after success-fully sitting the examination in London, an average of about fifty a year; between 1915 and 1924, just thirty-six sat and passed the examination, an average of less than four a year. The downturn is almost exactly coincident with the upsurge of mass protest in the subcontinent. After 1919 the imperial government could maintain the ICS at the requisite level only by, first, *nominating* Europeans to the Service and, secondly, by inducting, in increasing numbers, qualified Indians. This was despite a substantive improvement after 1924 in the conditions of elite service in India (for example, by the granting of more frequent leave and the offer of heavily subsidised passages to and from India for officers' wives and children). Over the period 1925–39, many more Indians than Europeans were appointed to the ICS, and of the Europeans who were sent out, almost half were the result of nomination – by implication a rather second-rate bunch. The long-term result of these recruitment difficulties was that the ICS evolved gradually from an almost exclusively European service into a mainly Indian cadre. This, of course, also had important implications for the 'steel frame' of British rule in India [78].

MACAULAY'S CHILDREN

In the early nineteenth century British officials and statesmen such as T.B. Macaulay conceived of a project to civilise India by implanting Western institutions there, in particular, parliamentary institutions. 'It may be', Macaulay told the House of Commons in July 1833, 'that ... by good government we may educate our subjects into a capacity for better government, that, having become instructed in European knowledge, they may, in some future age, demand European institutions. Whether such a day will ever come I know not. But never will I attempt to avert or retard it. Whenever it comes, it will be the proudest day in English history' [6 *p. 74*]. Now Macaulay was not anticipating a quick fix. Notice he says, 'in some future age'. But the successors of this reformist-minded generation were even less sanguine about the prospect of India's transformation. As we have seen, the generation of the 1890s were resigned to the virtual permanency of British rule in the subcontinent.

Nevertheless, the rulers could not ignore the progress that India had made, and was making, in the directions indicated by Macaulay as constituting the eventual goal of British rule. Every year the universities were turning out hundreds of Indian BAs and LLBs. By the late nineteenth century there was, undeniably, the makings of a Western-educated elite of 'brown Englishmen'. How should the Raj relate to these people? Was the growth of the Western-educated class a measure of the distance India had travelled towards fitness for self-rule? The officials of the day advanced three propositions by way of answer. The first, and perhaps most plausible, was that the educated elite constituted merely an 'infinitesimal' fraction of the population. The second was that the crop of university graduates which had so far emerged was insufficiently qualified to oversee the running of a large and complex administration. The third, and most contentious, was that the Western-educated were not the 'real' Indians, the ones for whom British rule had been constituted. 'The chief concern of the Government of India is to protect and foster the interests of the people of India', minuted the viceroy Lord Dufferin in 1888, 'and the people of India are not the seven or eight thousand students who have graduated at the universities, or the Pleaders [lawyers] recruited from their numbers in our Courts of Justice, or the newspaper writers, or the Europeanized• Zemindars, or the wealthy traders, but the voiceless millions whom neither education, nor civilization, nor the influence of European ideas of modern thought, have in the slightest degree transfigured or transformed from what their forefathers were a thousand years ago' [19 *p. 144*]. Once the cynosure of British hopes for their empire, Macaulay's civilising project was now an embarrassment, a 'deadly legacy' in Strachey's phrase [61 *p. 133*].

Compare this bleak assessment with the one handed down twenty years later in the *Report on Indian Constitutional Reform*, jointly authored by the secretary of state, Edwin Montagu, a Jewish Liberal, and the viceroy Lord Chelmsford, a Conservative peer and long-serving imperial proconsul. Although its substantive recommendations were rather cautious (an outcome which Montagu stoically attributed to the pernicious influence of Chelmsford's bureaucratic advisors), the report would have warmed Macaulay's heart. It reaffirmed that the ultimate purpose of British policy was to assist India towards self-government; it firmly repudiated the notion that the 'placid, pathetic contentment of the masses' should be the Raj's prime consideration; and it very specifically acknowledged an obligation to the urban intelligentsia. The English-educated, it opined gravely, were 'intellectually our children' [5 *p. 93*] [*Doc. 9*]. What pressures and circumstances caused this dramatic turnaround in imperial thinking?

THE DEVOLUTION OF POWER

In the aftermath of the Great Revolt of 1857, the government of India did some heavy soul-searching. The revolt had been a near disaster; and it had taken the imperial authorities very largely by surprise. Officials had reported stray protests against government orders, but this was dismissed as the carping of the odd few. Until the revolt broke, the British had no idea of the extent of up-country disaffection with their rule. The government's post-mortem focused, therefore, on rectifying perceived errors of policy and on devising strategies to ensure that it would never again find itself caught out by unforeseen developments.

One of the lessons drawn from the revolt was that the Raj had become too remote and had lost touch with what its subjects were thinking. Another was that the calamity might have been avoided if the disaffected had possessed another outlet (besides rebellion) for their grievances. These two perceptions coalesced into a plan to open up the government by inviting a small number of knowledgeable and influential non-officials to participate in its decision-making. In 1861 the legislative council of the governor-general was expanded to include between six and twelve 'additional' nominated members, and although the legislation did not make this mandatory, it was accepted that the majority of these nominees should always be Indians. Over time this number was broadened, to sixteen in 1892 and to sixty in 1909, while further places were opened up on the provincial councils of Bombay and Madras. Gradually, too, provision was made for some of the additional members to be elected – albeit on the basis of a restricted property, tax and educational franchise. Through this process of co-option, the government arguably widened its range of contacts with important elite sections of the population. In some cases, council membership converted outspoken critics into tacit supporters. But even where this did not occur, the councils performed a useful role as benign outlets for native opinion.

Meanwhile, the government found an additional reason to associate Indians with the administration: financial devolution. From the 1860s, the Raj suffered a succession of budgetary crises due, among other things, to the burgeoning cost of imperial defence. As a way of dealing with this problem, the central government from the 1870s began to devolve more of the responsibilities for policing, public works and other governmental activities on to the provincial governments in return for giving them an assigned share of existing taxes and the discretion to develop new sources of revenue tied to the delivery of specific services. However, the provinces remained in deficit and had to be baled out by periodic subventions from the centre. Then the Finance Department came up with a daring suggestion. Most Indian towns already possessed municipal corporations or councils; some districts had local rural boards as well. In almost all cases, these had Indian majorities. What if these councils and boards were given extra powers to raise money for local works, and at the same time were made responsible for their expenditure to an electorate of ratepayers? Such elected officials would be frugal with the taxpayers' money because waste would lead to them being swiftly ejected from office. More importantly still, the government would be relieved of the need to finance roads, parochial schools and other local works from imperial revenues. It would save the need to increase the income tax, an object of great odium. Last but not least, the devolution of limited powers to local governments posed little or no political risk. 'We shall not subvert the British Empire by allowing the Bengali Baboo to discuss his own schools and drains', quipped Finance Member Sir Evelyn Baring [60 *p. 1*]. The local self-government plan was put into operation by Lord Ripon in 1883. The results were so pleasing from an imperial viewpoint that, by 1918, Montagu and Chelmsford were prepared to apply the same logic to the provincial level of government, and to recommend the handing over of some developmental portfolios to Indian ministers responsible to an elected legislature.

By this time, however, the two original arguments for a limited devolution of power had been joined by a third: appeasement. As we have seen, the British by the late nineteenth century had become quite disenchanted with the English-educated and their pushy political agendas. But much as they might have liked to follow Curzon's lead and ignore the nationalist movement altogether, after 1905 they were compelled by its sheer size to take notice. Thereafter, debate within official circles centred on how best to contain the nationalist opposition, which in essence boiled down to a choice between repression and conciliation. In so far as the government's preference was for the latter, being cheaper and on the whole less likely to backfire, it found the issue of constitutional reform extremely useful as a bargaining chip. Moreover, the price of not granting at least some concessions as a sop to nationalist opinion was the risk that the movement might disavow its existing, rather moderate leaders and replace them with revolutionaries, men dedicated to the cult of the gun and the bomb, who would certainly settle for nothing less than a complete British withdrawal – a point that was pressed on the government by the moderates themselves at every opportunity. The necessity for conciliation, therefore, was not really questioned; the nub of the problem was to decide when to move and how much to give away.

Three times during the early twentieth century the imperial authorities were forced by the pressure of events to grapple with this thorny dilemma: between 1906 and 1909; between 1916 and 1919; and between 1927 and 1935. The first of these crises was occasioned by the backlash against Curzon's partition of Bengal and Sir Denzil Ibbotson's subsequent crackdown in the Punjab; but was affected also by a power struggle within the Congress movement between the 'moderate' and 'extremist' or New Party factions, which the moderates appeared, in 1906, to be losing. Anxious to do something to rescue the moderates, the viceroy, Lord Minto, though no democrat, proposed to London a scheme of reform 'framed on sufficiently liberal lines to satisfy the legitimate aspirations of all but the most advanced Indians' [69 *p. 139*]. It envisaged a modest increase in the size of the councils and in the number and powers of their non-official members, but ruled out direct voting from territorial constituencies. However, the home government in London came back almost at once with a much more radical scheme of its own. The general election of 1905 in Britain had returned a Liberal government and put a visionary reformer and former champion of Irish home rule, John Morley, into the Indian Office. Morley was also influenced by his friendship with and respect for the leading Congress moderate, Gopal Krishna Gokhale, who presented the secretary of state with a cogent and pragmatic argument for substantial democratic change. For three years the two sides batted the issue back and forth but eventually Morley prevailed. Under the Councils Act of 1909 the imperial legislative council was expanded to include sixty non-official members, twenty-seven of whom were to be elected from both territorial and special interest constituencies, while the provincial councils were enlarged sufficiently to create non-official majorities. As well, Morley used his discretion to appoint two Indians to his London-based panel of advisors, and urged Minto to do the same with regard to his own executive council. Minto obliged by appointing Satyendra Sinha, the advocate-general of Bengal, as his Law Member. For all their tokenism, these three nominations marked an important watershed, ending a hundred years of all-white colonial rule. Henceforward, high policy-making in India would always involve at least some Indian participation. Yet in other respects the 1909 reform package owed more to the thinking of the bureaucracy than to Morley's idealism. It restricted the right to vote to the very rich and privileged; it protected vested interests by reserving seats for landholders and chambers of commerce; and it drastically compromised the democratic principle that all votes should be of equal worth by creating separate electorates specially for Muslims and fixing a lower property and educational qualification for Muslim voters. Gokhale put on a brave face, but he was bitterly disappointed.

The next imperial initiative in the matter of reform took place in the middle of the First World War and was directly consequent upon the millenarian hopes, social tensions and political shifts triggered by India's substantial material contribution to the Entente cause. By the third year of the war, 1916, nationalism was once again snapping hard at the heels of the Raj. A reunited Congress had lifted its demands and was now calling for an early grant of self-government within the Empire on the model of the white dominions. More worrying still, it had settled its earlier differences with the Muslims. For the time being the Raj could not count on keeping control by exploiting the country's religious animosities. And there were other threats too, in the shape of the mass-based Home Rule Leagues which had mushroomed in Bombay and Madras, modelled after Ireland's Sinn Fein, and the clandestine Sikh Ghadr ('Mutiny') Party, which, according to police reports, was hoping to liberate India with German assistance. As for the moderates, the faction had become almost moribund following the death of its two best leaders, Gokhale and Pherozeshah Mehta, in 1915. Nevertheless, faced with adversaries on so many fronts, the British felt they had no choice but to play, once again, the appeasement card. 'The vital question for us is, will the Moderates rally to the side of Government and show some political courage and powers of resistance, if Government does disclose a policy which can be weighed, article for article, against the manifestos of the Extremists?', pondered the United Provinces' Sir James Meston. 'Many of my Indian friends think that they will, but that no time should be lost in calling upon them' [38 *p. 195*]. But what should this policy pronouncement say? Viceroy Chelmsford's view was that only a bold and imaginative statement, setting out where British policy in India was headed, would suffice. After consulting his governors (Meston among them), he sent a draft text to London for consideration. It characterised the goal of British policy as 'the endowment of British India, as an integral part of the Empire, with self-government', an ambiguous pledge which was further qualified by the imposition of prerequisites, such as the 'wide diffusion of education, [and] the softening of racial and religious differences' [59 *p. 55*]. At first London was unenthusiastic, but their attitude underwent an abrupt about-face with the arrival of Edwin Montagu at the India Office in July 1917. By August Montagu had persuaded his Cabinet colleagues to agree, not only to a firm statement of intent, but to a further liberalisation of the constitution in directions to be negotiated between himself and Chelmsford over the winter of 1917–18. Moreover, thanks to the obstinacy of the former viceroy, and now foreign secretary, Lord Curzon, who insisted on the substitution of 'responsible government' for 'self-government' (apparently unaware that the former term had a quite specific and far-reaching parliamentary application), the famous declaration of 20 August 1917 actually went beyond what its original authors had intended. Britain was now implicitly committed to allowing Indians to rule themselves [*Doc. 10*]. Three years later part of that pledge was redeemed with the passage of the Government of India Act of 1919. The Act set up a new, 200-seat, bicameral legislature at the centre and further expanded the provincial legislatures; it endowed all these with elective majorities; it enfranchised, in total, about six million Indians, or about one-tenth of the adult male population; as noted above, it provided for partial ministerial responsibility in the provinces, the system known as 'dyarchy'; and to the dismay of many, it maintained, and indeed extended, the principle of separate electorates for minorities.

The third great imperial debate about the ends and means of reform was triggered by the clause in the Act of 1919 which stipulated that the constitutional question had to be revisited no later than 1929. In a bid to hijack the process while they were still in office, the Conservatives in 1927 sent a parliamentary delegation under Sir John Simon out to India to investigate how the current arrangements were working and to advise on how they might be improved. But before the Simon Commission could complete its report two things intervened. First, a general election in Britain put the Labour Party into office. Labour was much more committed than the Conservatives to the nominal British goal of preparing India for self-rule within the Empire. Secondly, the Congress at the end of 1928 put the government on notice that it would launch all-out civil disobedience unless India was granted internal self-government (equivalent to what was then being described in imperial circles as 'dominion status') by the end of the following year. In an attempt to avert this looming showdown, the viceroy, Lord Irwin, borrowed a leaf out of Montagu's book. He proposed to London a statement confirming that Britain's goal for India was indeed dominionhood. In the light of the watershed Balfour Declaration of 1926, this was tantamount to a promise of full internal self-government. Labour prime minister Ramsay MacDonald welcomed this suggestion, and in October 1929 the 'Irwin Declaration' was published. As well as clarifying the dominion status issue, it informed the Indian politicians and public that the government intended to invite all interested parties to a Round Table

Conference (RTC) to devise, independently of the Simon Commission, a constitutional framework for the future Indian dominion. In the event, the RTC opened in 1930 without the initial participation of the Congress, which refused to go back on its ultimatum. Nevertheless, despite, or perhaps because of, the absence of Congress, by 1931 a broad measure of agreement had been reached as to the shape and powers of the new state. It would be a federation of the provinces and the Indian states, and it would be sub-stantially (though not completely) self-governing. Four years later, having been fine-tuned by two more conferences and a joint select committee of parliament, this scheme received royal assent as the Government of India Act, 1935. While keeping back some powers at the centre, it gave the provinces a very large measure of responsible government, and it conferred the right to vote on some 36 million people India-wide, women as well as men, about one-sixth of the total adult population.

The British liberalised their governance of India grudgingly and with grave reservations. As late as the 1930s, many senior officials in India, such as Army Commander-in-Chief General Sir Philip Chetwode, remained entirely opposed to any political advance for fear that it would lead to chaos [*Doc. 11*]. Nor did they embark on the process of devolution as a means of preparing India for self-government (at least as the term was understood by the Indian nationalists). Even John Morley, progressive Liberal that he was, categorised the notion that his reforms were intended to lay the foundations for a parliamentary system in India as a 'fantastic and ludicrous dream' [57 *p. 73*]. When, after 1917, the British expanded their policy horizon to embrace 'responsible government' for India, they did so on the specific understanding that the country would remain an 'integral' part of the British Empire.

Yet there was an inexorable logic to devolution that the British could not escape. With each concession, some ground was lost. By the 1930s, the constitutional reform process, in conjunction with the steady Indianisation of the ICS, had appreciably (some might say significantly) weakened the Raj's grip on the subcontinent. This limited the demands the imperial authorities could make, further reducing its value as an exploitable resource. Moreover, once started the process was well-nigh irreversible. Each instal-ment of reform raised client expectations, whetted Indian appetites for freedom. These rising expectations could only be met by blanket repression (at best, only a temporary option) or further concessions, leading to a further erosion of authority. Back when the government was still wondering about the propriety of Indians voting for municipal councils, Finance Member Sir Evelyn Baring made an astute observation: 'When once the ball of political reform is set rolling, it is apt to gather speed as it goes' [61 *p. 161*]. By the 1930s, it was travelling very fast indeed.

CHAPTER THREE

NATIONALISM

All governments survive in the long run by satisfying the needs and wants of their citizenry. The Raj began to stumble when, towards the end of the nineteenth century, fiscal constraints and imperial responsibilities forced it to cut back on programmes and services which the middle class, especially, had come to rely on for their economic well-being.

As already remarked, the mid-nineteenth century witnessed the emergence of a considerable body of English-knowing, and more generally Western-educated, Indians. In 1881 some 150,000 pupils were receiving education in British India in 'English Arts' colleges or secondary schools; by 1901 their number had swelled to over 420,000. During the same period, about 30,000 of these college boys went on to graduate from university. To be sure, the half million or so English-educated Indians living at the turn of the century represented (as the government was fond of pointing out) only a miniscule fraction of society. But they dominated the professions, in particular the law and the public service, but also medicine, journalism and teaching. It was in the best interest of the British to keep this articulate and influential group happy. Increasingly, they were unsuccessful.

The root of the malaise lay in the education system itself. British India's colleges and universities had, by modern standards, collossal failure rates. Out of 24,000 candidates who sat for the matriculation examination in 1881, just 11,000 passed. Around 1914 the pass rates for the BA and BSc degrees were running at 62 per cent in Madras, 43 per cent in United Provinces, just 35 per cent in the Punjab. While most of the unsuccessful candidates probably had only themselves to blame, this did not in any way lessen the burden of their disappointment. However, the greater problem was the increasing inability of the public service and the professions to offer employment suitable to the needs and aspirations of the Western-educated – even those among them who had graduated successfully. At the top level, the ICS had been opened up, in principle, to Indians, by the Queen's proclamation of 1858. However, various, not entirely accidental, impediments (the fact that the annual entrance examination was held in London, the requirement from the 1870s for candidates to have had two years at an English university, the lowering of the maximum age of entry during the same period from twenty-three to nineteen) kept the intake of Indian civilians to a trickle until the 1920s. In 1885 there were just sixteen Indians in a Service over 900-strong. More generally, the top positions in the Statutory and Provincial Services, the levels of the elite bureaucracy especially earmarked for Indians, were far too few to absorb the supply of qualified men being churned out yearly by the educational system. Many had to make do with more poorly paid jobs lower down – or none at all. And it was the same with the legal profession. A few Indians in the late nineteenth century became extremely rich working as barristers in the chief Presidency courts. Badruddin Tyabji, an eminent Muslim lawyer from Bombay, earned 122,000 rupees from his legal practice in 1890, which was four times the annual salary of an ICS officer. But most law graduates had to graft a living working as *vakils* (pleaders) in *mofussil* (provincial) towns. In Madras, just 267 lawyers (most of them city lawyers) were earning incomes of over 2,000 rupees annually in 1890; of the rest, some were pulling in as little as 500 rupees a year. As early as 1884 Ripon saw the menace lurking on the horizon: 'Unless we are prepared to afford these men legitimate openings for their aspirations and ambitions, we had better at once abolish our Universities and close our Colleges, for they will only serve to turn out year by year in ever-increasing numbers men who must inevitably become the most dangerous and influential enemies of our rule' [61 *p. 148*]. But the British did neither, and the problem continued to grow. For every satiated professional man at the end of the nineteenth century, a dozen others harboured feelings of disappointment and frustration, feelings that a little propaganda could easily turn into anger and resentment against the government.

Another source of Indian discontent was taxation. The government's tax take rose from 374 million rupees in 1872 to 501 million rupees in 1893, an increase of over one-third. Much of this fell on the urban middle class, in part because it was a big consumer of imported goods and liquor (subject to customs duties and excise tax, respectively) and the major recipient of salaries and fees (which were subject to income tax), but mainly because the government was loath to risk unsettling the countryside by jacking up the land revenue. (Land taxes rose during the latter nineteenth century, but much less than agricultural prices.)

Taxpayer resentment was sharpened, too, by the fiscal critiques of writers such as English radical William Digby and retired Bengali divisional commissioner Romesh Chandra Dutt [*Doc. 12*], which suggested that they were not getting value from the government for their tax dollars. By the

1890s, about 30 per cent of the government's expenditure each year went to support the Indian Army; approximately another 10 per cent was soaked up by the police budget and a further 25 per cent by the costs of the bureaucracy (including collection charges). Much of the remainder was used to meet the aforementioned Home Charges, whose real burden increased yearly as the value of the silver rupee declined in relation to gold-standard sterling. By contrast, welfare and development areas (public works, education, health and agricultural research) together comprised less than 10 per cent of outlays. These stark figures were so damning in themselves, that they hardly needed any embellishment from the government's critics. However Dutt and Digby made the further telling point that the government was costly precisely because it was an English government. Was any viceroy, they challenged, worth £17,000 a year? Were the much-vaunted ICS really up to their £3,000 a year salaries and £1,000 a year pensions for life? Could poor India afford such an expensive government? The more these issues were aired in books, in the press and on the public platform, the more educated Indians responded with an emphatic 'no'.

Meanwhile (as the budget figures testify), the Raj was imposing itself on the common people in a way no previous government – even the government of the English East India Company – had done. To be fair, some of this new bureaucratic penetration of society had, on the surface at least, an altruistic motive: for instance, the organisation of government work camps under the Famine Code and schemes to provide free vaccination against disease, both of which were intended to (and did) save lives. But the public remained deeply suspicious. Many interpreted the government's interest as a cloak for the gathering of information about their wealth (for tax purposes), or as part of an agenda to wean them away from their ancestral beliefs and customs. When bubonic plague broke out in the Bombay presidency in 1896, the government moved (as it thought, sensibly) to isolate carriers through the imposition of strict quarantine procedures. But these measures proved very unpopular, especially in Poona (Pune). The British officers responsible for implementing them were accused of brutality, violating the sanctity of temples and *purdah* (womens') quarters, even of spreading the disease deliberately for some nefarious purpose of their own [*Doc. 13*]. This popular backlash culminated, as previously noted, with the assassination in 1897 of the British Plague Commissioner in Poona, Rand, but resentment among high-caste Hindus continued to simmer long after his death and the subsequent execution of his youthful killer.

However, nothing in the late nineteenth century cast such a shadow over the Raj's claim to be a good government, or excited so much anger among its subjects, as racism. The most common, overt and downright ugly form of white racism was assault – verbal abuse and physical attacks on lower-class Indians by plantation foremen, white masters and mistresses of households, and drunken European soldiers. Mostly these went unreported, or were covered up, yet patchy as it is, the official record lists 81 Indians as having been killed by whites in shooting incidents between 1880 and 1900. But racism was also, more insidiously, entrenched in British administrative practice. We have already referred to the obstacles that were placed in the way of Indians joining the ICS. Until the end of the First World War, Indians were denied King's commissions in the Indian Army. In 1883 Sir Courtney Ilbert's Bill to end the legal convention whereby Europeans accused of crimes could elect not to be tried by Indian judges caused such an outcry among the white population of Calcutta that the government was forced to withdraw it and substitute a drastically watered-down proposal. Until almost the end of the Raj, Indians were banned from many elite recreational clubs, and, until 1914, they were not permitted to walk on the main street of Simla, the Mall. And the racial divide informed pay ·structures as well. On the railways, Indians got two-thirds less than Europeans for doing similar jobs (and less, too, than 'Anglo-Indians', people of mixed race). Last but not least, the scales of justice in British Indian courts were weighted subtly but perceptibly in favour of the whites. Bengali poet and novelist Rabindranath Tagore mused bleakly that an Englishman could probably hit him with impunity, because 'I am merely an individual, while he ... stands for the power of the state. ... And if I [were to] hit an Englishman, the judge would consider it an attack on the authority of the state, as undermining English prestige' [45 *p. 69*]. Tagore's supposition is born out by how few of the aforementioned assaults on Indians resulted in convictions appropriate to the crime. In one celebrated case, in 1904, the aide-de-camp to the lieutenant-governor of Bengal, Lord Ampthill, was tried on a charge of manslaughter for wilfully causing the death of a servant. The servant's spleen had ruptured after his master had administered a hefty kick by way of rebuke for some spilled coffee. The judge – a fellow European of course – found the ADC guilty of a 'push with the foot', and fined him the equivalent of a month's salary.

Some Indians, like Damodar Chapekar, sought revenge for the injustices handed out by British rule in violence; others, like Tagore and Romesh Dutt, hit back with their brains and their pens; others again threw themselves into the task of organising a credible and effective movement of nationalist resistance to British colonialism. One of the latter was Surendranath Banerjea.

Born in 1848 into a *bhadralok* family, Banerjea aspired, like so many of his caste and generation, to join the ICS; this required him, while still a teenager, to travel to England to study for the examination, a venture that was both enormously expensive for his family and a risk to his social health, since in those days crossing the ocean was considered a polluting thing by orthodox Hindus. When he left, his mother wept bitter tears, never expecting to see her son again. However, the young Bengali answered every challenge, passed near the top of his class, returned safely, and was duly admitted into the Service. Then, with success apparently at his feet, Banerjea's troubles began. Almost immediately, there was a move to disqualify him on the grounds that he had lied about his age on his application form. He contested this bureaucratic slander in the courts, and won. The next setback came three years later. Put to work as an assistant district officer under an unsympathetic superior, he fudged some paperwork. It was the sort of thing civil servants did all the time, and should have earned him a reprimand; instead he was summarily dismissed from the Service. Hurt but unbowed, Banerjea now elected to try for a career in the law. Again he went to England, studied and successfully sat the examinations. But the old white boy network stood firm; he was refused permission to join the bar. Very disillusioned and angry, Banerjea nevertheless managed to rationalise what had happened to him. He had been victimised by an evil system. 'The personal wrong done to me was an illustration of the helpless impotency of my people' [23 *p. 30*]. He turned his considerable talents to teaching and journalism, using these professions as platforms to push his message of national awakening. For instance, he aroused his students by telling them romantic stories about the triumphant Italian unification movement, which invariably ended with the following challenge: 'Who amongst you will be a Mazzini, who a Garibaldi?' In 1876 Surendranath Banerjea established the country's first truly modern political organisation, the Indian Association of Calcutta. In 1883, as the Ilbert Bill controversy raged, he successfully fought a defamation case against a prominent member of the British community, earning himself the sobriquet 'Surrender-Not'. By 1885 Banerjea had achieved far more fame as a nationalist than he ever could have done as a servant of the Raj.

Surendranath Banerjea's story was by no means unique. Many Indians turned to nationalism after suffering personal loss and humiliation as a result of official discrimination, and some of them would become, like Banerjea, prominent nationalist leaders. Aurobindo Ghose and Subhas Chandra Bose are two that come readily to mind. Indeed, the frustrated careerist is such a common figure in nationalist iconography that one is tempted to ask 'what if...?' But that would be pointless, not simply because the movement was greater than any few of its individual leaders, but because the motivations of the Banerjeas and the Ghoses went far beyond simple revenge. Official discrimination might have got them started, but what drove them on was their belief in a grand and powerful idea, the India of national self-determination.

NATIONALIST IMAGININGS

The nation-state was born in pre-modern Europe. Similarly, nationalism, the doctrine that promotes and justifies nation-building, is a creation of European thought. While (emulating their European counterparts) Indian nationalists would later support their demands for self-determination by appeals to history and tradition, invoking in particular the golden-age myth of an ancient common culture underpinned by the beliefs and rituals of Hinduism, India was not in any objective sense a nation before the coming of British rule; nor, indeed, even then. What occurred in the latter nineteenth century was not so much a sudden welding together of the subcontinent's disparate peoples – although something of that nature did occur, as we shall see, on a limited scale – but rather a transformation in the way Indians thought about their identity. India, like Earl Canning's New World, was 'called into existence' to serve a purpose. The purpose was freeing India from British control.

During the third quarter of the nineteenth century, educated men in Calcutta, Bombay and other big cities came to understand that if India was ever to secure its freedom, the first essential prerequisite was the creation of an organisation capable of holding a dialogue with the Raj, one that could not be dismissed out of hand as a casual debating club or discredited as a vehicle of sectional interests. Since the Raj was subcontinental in its extent and reach, and claimed to speak equally for all classes and communities, this counter-Raj would also, they realised, need to be both multi-communal and all-Indian. This assumption informed Banerjea's founding of the *Indian* Association, which although based in Calcutta had branches in other parts of Bengal and was intended eventually to reach out into other provinces. It was certainly integral to the project that superseded Banerjea's a few years later, the Indian National Congress.

Notice, however, that the latter organisation, as well as laying claims to be all-Indian, was also advertising itself as a *national* forum. This, too, was no accident. The appropriation of that pregnant term signalled the intention of the Congress, not merely to confront the Raj, but to challenge its legitimacy.

By the nineteenth century, nationality was already a sanctified principle in Europe (particularly Western Europe) and America. Accordingly, the idea became a part of the cultural baggage exported to India with British colonialism, along with notions about the rights of the individual, equality before the law, and representative government – all in their way equally subversive. Without, it seems, being openly conscious of the irony, the British, through their education system, planted and nourished in the Indian mind the firm conviction that the proper constituency of the modern state was nationality.

But then, the Indians hardly needed their British schoolmasters to tell them about nation-building. Many successful examples of the process were there to be seen – not only Britain itself, but also the United States, Italy and Germany – and indications were, more would follow. Nationalism, and its corollary, 'national self-determination', was the cult of the age. British prime minister, Welshman David Lloyd George, spoke of it approvingly, while American president Woodrow Wilson in 1918 made it one of his country's war aims and argued for the principle to be applied in any Allied post-war settlement, a point not lost on Surendranath Banerjea watching intently from Calcutta. 'They are talking [in Britain] about what will happen after the war in Canada, in Australia. ... May we not also talk about it a little from our standpoint? Are we to be charged with embarrassing the Government when we follow the examples of illustrious public men, men weighted with a sense of responsibility at least as onerous as that felt by our critics and candid friends?' [38 *p. 190*]. By the early twentieth century, then, Indians could advance a claim to national self-determination confident that the concept was solidly grounded both in historical precedent and in Western political discourse.

However there was a sticking point; first they had to prove to the British, the world (and not least to themselves), that India was actually a nation as the term was conventionally understood.

In 1888, three years after the foundation of the Indian National Congress, Sir John Strachey opined confidently 'that men of the Punjab, Bengal, the North-West Provinces and Madras should ever feel that they belong to one great Indian nation, is impossible' [33 *p. 8*]. It is easy to understand how he came to that conclusion. India was vast. Its people spoke a dozen languages and innumerable dialects. They were Hindus, but also Muslims, Sikhs, Christians and Buddhists. The Hindus alone were divided into at least 3,000 discrete castes. But Strachey failed to realise two things. The first is that the disparate and far-flung regions of the subcontinent were slowly but surely being knitted together by technology and bureaucracy. We have already remarked on the rapid spread of the railway network and the postal service in the latter nineteenth century and their mushrooming popularity with the public. These services allowed Indians, for the first time, to communicate with each other easily and quickly over long distances. In addition, railway travel allowed Indians to witness and experience at first hand life outside their own town and province. Growing familiarity with the subcontinent made its distances seem less daunting, its myriad landscapes less strange. Separated by speech and dress, Bengalis and Punjabis, Marathas and Madrasis, began to find, somewhat to their suprise, that they nevertheless had some things (core values, ideas, basic racial characteristics) in common. Conversely, travelling overseas (which over a million Indians did between 1914 and 1919 in the course of their war service) underlined how similar all Indians were in relation to peoples of other lands.

But if the rail system facilitated communication and assisted in the spread of national awareness, the printing press did so on an even grander scale, for it put the published word within reach of the masses. Take the example of newpapers. The first broadsheet to use the new technology made its appearance in Calcutta in 1823. By 1905 over 1,300 papers were being published across India on a daily or weekly basis, about half in English and half in the vernaculars. Total circulation was around two million, while the more expensive English papers sold about 275,000 copies per issue. However, the impact of the press on the Indian mind went far beyond what even these not inconsiderable figures would suggest. Contemporary reports indicate that single copies of newspapers frequently passed through many literate hands. More importantly still, there are numerous accounts of newspapers being read aloud under street lamps or the shade of trees to crowds of eager listeners. Illiteracy *was* a barrier to written communication in India, but not as big a one as we might think. As for bureaucracy, the obvious point to make here is that, while there might not have been an Indian nation in the late nineteenth century, there was already an 'Indian' state – the Raj. This was a fact of great symbolic value. But British rule also assisted the process of national integration in more concrete ways as well. For instance, English-language education provided the country's provincial intelligentsia with a *lingua franca* and, to some extent, a common philosophical framework, one which, moreover, included many elements conducive to the development of a consciousness of nationality. Equally important was the administrative impact of the Raj, which exposed the subcontinent's diverse regions to the homogenising influence of uniform policies, rules and procedures.

Strachey's other mistake (although an understandable one, in the light of his background and the thinking of the period) was to assume that India lacked the essential prerequisites for nationhood. He assumed, along with most people in the nineteenth century, that nationality was an objective condition, a product of race, language, religion and custom, and that no people could aspire to nationhood who were not, to a large degree, ethnically homogeneous – an hypothesis that of course fitted nicely with the European situation at that time. When Strachey applied that hypothesis to India, he was driven to only one conclusion. Fragmented, socially divided India might in time give birth to many nations, but never to a single nation co-extensive with the subcontinent. However, the hypothesis was wrong. At least since the 1980s, scholars have come to believe (in part as a response to the increasing tendency for nations to be created on the basis of a single criterion of affiliation – such as religion or some form of religiously-mandated culture) that they are not so much natural artifacts as expressions of political will, 'imagined communities' in Benedict Anderson's evocative term [36]. In the light of this modern perspective, we can see that ultimately it did not matter, as Strachey thought, that India lacked homogeneity. Rather, the crucial thing was whether the Indian provincial elites possessed the will and the ability to transcend their social and linguistic differences, and to imagine themselves as a political collectivity. One has only to look at the editorials in the native press of the period to see that this process of creative imagining was already well under way by the 1880s [*Doc. 14*]. Nevertheless, it would take decades of organisational effort by the elites to sell this vision to the putative national membership, people who were not only profoundly diverse but who had mostly never met each other face to face.

CHRISTMAS *TAMASHAS*

By 1885 the idea of Indian nationality had taken firm root in the minds of the urban intelligentsia. On 28 December of that year, responding to a call by retired ICS officer, celebrated ornithologist and nationalist sympathiser A.O. Hume, seventy-three men of this class met at Bombay under the chairmanship of W.C. Bonnerjee, a Calcutta lawyer, to establish a forum for the discussion and promotion of the nationality question. The new organisation was called, appropriately, the Indian National Congress (INC).

During the first thirty years of its existence the goals, methods and achievements of the INC were quite limited. According to Hume, often described as the 'founder' of the Congress, its objects were, first, to promote the 'fusion' of the peoples of the subcontinent into one nation, secondly, to work for the social and 'moral' 'regeneration' of the country and, thirdly, to help consolidate the 'union between England and India' by lobbying for the reform of those features of the administration of the Raj 'as may be unjust or injurious' to Indians. But initially, most of its energies were focused on the third of these objectives, and then only within a rather narrow sphere. In monetary terms, its chief activity was maintaining an office in London, which was rightly seen as the focal point of British policy-making and the place where Indians were most likely to receive a sympathetic hearing. On the propaganda front, most of the resolutions passed at the early Congress sessions took the form of cautious appeals to the British to lower taxation and increase Indian participation in the government by expanding the elective element in the legislative councils and allowing local candidates to sit the ICS examination in India. The emphasis was firmly on constitutional reform within a continuing imperial structure. Conversely, the INC fervently denied that it had any intention of trying to challenge the Raj's mandate to rule; indeed, its leaders constantly reiterated Hume's theme that Congress was a bulwark of that rule. In his presidential speech of 1886, the Parsi Dadabhai Naoroji asked his audience rhetorically whether the Congress could be described as a 'nursery for sedition'. 'No, no', came the deafening response [57 *p. 43*]. This cooperative stance was reflected, too, in the openness of the organisation to white membership. Between 1885 and 1917 four Englishmen (and one woman) served terms as Congress president, while Hume was the body's *de facto* chief executive for over ten years.

As for the other foundational goals of the Congress, social regeneration and consciousness-raising, the former immediately ran into resistance from passionate secularists, who believed that religious issues should have no place in politics, and pragmatists who felt (probably rightly) that social issues (such as the vexed question of child marriage) would be divisive and therefore damaging to the greater national cause. After a brief flirtation with the idea of setting up a parallel National Social Conference, the Congress leaders decided that the only sensible and politically viable course was to drop social reform altogether from their agenda. And the latter, raising national consciousness, although it remained very much at the centre of the INC's programme, was compromised by the organisation's limited reach into the hinterland and heartland of the country. Until 1899 it had no formal constitution, and for its first two decades of life little real presence apart from the annual plenary sessions (which were usually held at the end of the year to take advantage of the cold weather season and the Christmas public holidays). More to the point, it lacked a structure of sub-provincial and local branches to carry its message to the masses.

But more than this could hardly have been expected from the type of men who ran the early Congress. The overwhelming majority were men from the bourgeoisie, big-city professionals with a sprinkling of merchants and rural landowners. Eleven of the first sixteen Congress presidents were barristers. And not from the *petit-bourgeoisie* either. When young Jawaharlal Nehru arrived at the 1912 Bankipore meeting, he found himself in the midst of a sea of 'morning coats and pressed trousers' [31 *p. 27*]. The Bombay lawyer Pherozeshah Mehta reserved an entire carriage for himself and his retinue for the cross-country journey to the Calcutta session of 1901. At the same session, Gandhi, visiting from South Africa, watched with amazement as a Brahmin delegate from Calcutta had his shirt buttoned up by a bearer, while Poona's M.G. Ranade was once seen in public attended by 'about ... twenty-five coolies' [54 *p. 64*]. Jawaharlal's father, Motilal, another hugely successful high court lawyer, lived at Allahabad in a mansion lit by electricity and drove a motor car when there were just a handful in the country. It was sometimes alleged, only half in jest, that he sent his laundry to be washed in Paris. While there was perhaps no inherent contradiction in the fact that these avowed patriots were by and large very wealthy, their wealth and elevated social position (many were Brahmins) placed limitations on the form that patriotism took. Such men might consider getting rid of the British, but they were wedded to the system of property and fearful of sponsoring anything that might upset the social equilibrium. They did not understand, nor were they at ease, with those whom Banerjea called 'the lower classes' [54 *p. 69*]. Arguably, what commended the Congress to this elite was that it provided a means of 'getting hold of' and politically educating the 'great lower middle classes' before the latter fell into the hands of 'reckless demagogues' bent on revolution [*Doc. 15*].

Was the Congress, then, simply a footnote to the history of the period? In some ways it was. As we have seen, it suffered both from structural weaknesses and ideological contradictions. As well as being elitist, its membership was quite small compared with that of other contemporary organisations such as the Arya Samaj (Aryan Society) or the Gaurakshini Sabha (Association for Cow Protection), whose activities played such a vital role in the revivalist movement described later in the chapter. So little disturbance did it create to the workings of the administration (at least until 1905), that the government on occasions found itself half-believing Hume's argument that the outlet for the moderate ventilation of grievances that Congress provided was actually beneficial to the health of the Indian Empire. Indeed, it may not be too unfair to suggest that even the party faithful, during this era, did not see the organisation as central to their lives. When the time for the annual December gathering came round, Congress stalwarts would joke that they were off to the 'Christmas *tamasha*'. A *tamasha* is a public entertainment. Western-style politics was still, at this time, a leisure activity for people with the time and means for self-indulgence.

But the foregoing analysis, while factually correct, probably does insufficient justice to the symbolic importance of the early Congress, first as a sign to other Indians and, secondly, as a signal to the government. Even as they sought to dismiss the Congress as the vehicle of a 'microscopic minority', the British realised that its foundation marked the beginning of a new era in their relationship with the Indian people, an era in which their right to rule would be increasingly contested. Also, while its deficiencies lingered, the Congress did evolve. It grew gradually more confident and more broadly based. From seventy-three at Bombay in 1885, the number of delegates rose to 607 at the Madras session of 1887 and to 1,248 at the Allahabad session of 1888. Thereafter, until the end of the century, the number never dropped below 500. Many more people, besides, helped choose the delegates, or belonged to associations that sent delegates, or read press reports about the proceedings. One Congress report from the 1880s suggested that this number might have been as high as fifteen million. Last but not least, the Congress began slowly to take on board some wider political concerns and attitudes, which gave its agenda, for the first time, a militant edge.

Grassroots politics in India is often represented as a post-Gandhian phenomenon, a development of the twentieth century. This is only half true. In the sense that politics is about the pursuit of power, there had always been politics of a kind in village India. But these local power struggles had remained, for the most part, local. They had never had a significant impact on the politics of the Indian courts. For centuries, commoners and kings had waged separate struggles, each indifferent to the fate of the other. Towards the end of the nineteenth century, however, a few far-sighted modern leaders, conscious of the latent power that dwelt, untapped, in the subcontinent's myriad villages, started to build bridges with the masses in a bid to mobilise them for the national cause.

This was not an easy task. Although the villages were less isolated from the broader currents of Indian life than they had been in former centuries, the peasantry remained, very naturally, fixated on their own life-and-death concerns; issues of nationality, constitutional reform and political freedom were wholly beyond their grasp, and seemingly irrelevant to their immediate situation. How could the needs and aspirations of the national struggle be brought home to these parochial minds? The problem was solved initially by a brilliant Poona Brahmin politician named Bal Gangadhar Tilak. He solved it by tapping into the folk culture of his region, Maharashtra. In 1893 Tilak re-energised the annual Maharashtrian festival in honour of the elephant-headed god, Ganesh, and turned it into a forum for anti-British propaganda dressed up as Hindu mythology. Three years later, he started a new festival in celebration of the region's greatest folk-hero, the seventeenth-century Hindu warrior-king Shivaji. This allowed him to make even more explicitly anti-British points by way of analogy with Shivaji's successful revolt against the 'foreign' rule of the Mughals [*Doc. 16*].

But Tilak was not by any means just a manipulator of Indian tradition for political ends. He was a deeply orthodox man who had already acquired renown as an interpreter of the *Bhagavad Gita*, the bible of Vaishnava Hinduism. And the same was true of the politicians who followed in his footsteps, such as Bengal's Aurobindo Ghose and the Punjab's Lala Lajpat Rai. Partly in response to the missionary challenge of Protestant Christianity, Hinduism was going through a phase of critical self-examination and renewal. Where, earlier in the century, Hindu intellectuals such as Rammohun Roy had attacked traditional Hinduism for harbouring 'irrational' superstitions, pride in the ancient religion of the *Vedas* was once again in the ascendant – even the 'worship' of 'sacred' cows was no longer considered, in polite Hindu circles, a matter for apology. The abject Hindu had turned, and now, increasingly, it was Christianity, and more generally Western civilisation, that found itself the target of polite condescension. In

1893 Swami Vivekananda astounded the World Parliament of Religions at Chicago by proclaiming the triumph of 'Indian spirituality' over Western materialism. Arya Samaj leader Lajpat Rai, Tilak and Aurobindo all embraced this movement of religious awakening warmly, in part because it allowed them to reassert their cultural identity as Indians after years of exposure to Western education and, in Aurobindo's case, years spent abroad. Significantly, Lajpat was also a product of a very oecumenical – or possibly culturally confused – household, in which Western ideas competed with Jain and Islamic influences.

Hindu 'revivalism' as channelled through the speeches and writings of Tilak, Lajpat and Aurobindo permanently changed the milieu of Indian politics. From this time onwards, the vocabulary of public discourse was increasingly coloured by Hindu words, symbols and stories. An early expression of this trend was the adoption of the hymn *Bande Mataram* ('Hail to the Mother') as the Congress anthem. Composed as an ode to Bengal by Bankim Chandra Chatterjee, the song is also, by implication, an invocation of the earth-mother goddess, and the fourth verse refers specifically to Durga, wife of Shiva, and Lakshmi, the goddess of wealth. Later, Gandhi took this use of symbolic language a step further when he described the goal Congress was working towards as 'Ram raj', the rule of Rama, an allusion familiar to all Hindus from the popular *Ramayana* story.

In the short term, however, the crucial contribution of the Tilak– Lajpat–Aurobindo faction was to shake up an increasingly moribund Congress. At the turn of the twentieth century, Congress was still tightly controlled by a small oligarchy which included, most notably, Gokhale, Mehta, Motilal Nehru and Sir Dinshaw Wacha who had taken over from Hume as general secretary. These leaders remained wedded to Hume's 'moderate' programme, which is to say that their ambition remained, primarily, the conservative one of securing a fair share of political power for Indians within the existing imperial structure. The New Party or 'Extremists' (as the dissident group now came to be known), knew no such inhibitions. They were fiercely dedicated to the goal of total freedom, which, typically, they referred to by its Indian name, *swaraj* ('our rule'). '*Swaraj* is my birthright, and I will have it', thundered Tilak [52 *p. 115*]. Nor, unlike the ruling oligarchy, did the New Party feel constrained to work only through officially approved channels. Rather, they called upon the Congress to start using extra-constitutional methods, such as boycott and mass agitation, to press its demands. Foreshadowing Gandhi, Tilak even flirted with the idea of mass civil disobedience, telling a crowd at Calcutta that if they acted unitedly and steadfastly enough, they could bring the government to its knees 'tomorrow' by refusing to pay taxes.

The New Party's uncompromising patriotism, dressed up in language that recalled the glory of the ancient Hindu past, struck an immediate chord with the youth of the country. When Tilak visited Calcutta in 1906, a crowd of 25,000 turned out to hear him speak, many of them university and college students. The Extremists benefited, too, by the growing disenchantment with British rule, which intensified in the first years of the new century in reaction to the blight of famine and to the hard-nosed policies of Lord Curzon. When Curzon in 1904 announced his scheme for the creation of a new province of East Bengal, the Moderates were no less dismayed than most other sections of middle-class Hindu society; but they had no remedies to propose beyond the old ones of remonstrance and petition, which looked in the circumstances hopelessly inadequate. By contrast, the New Party had a programme of action, which included picketing of government offices and liquor shops, but whose centrepiece was a boycott of British goods in favour of local produce, or *swadeshi* ('of our country'). Characteristically, *swadeshi* was represented not merely as a patriotic duty, but also a religious duty. Following Surendranath Banerjea's lead, and at the urging of their priests, thousands of Bengalis took vows in temples to buy only *swadeshi* merchandise. In addition, social sanctions, such as the boycotting of foreign cloth by laundrymen, and the withholding of religious rites from villagers seen wearing it, were used to enforce compliance. The campaign was so successful that, by 1906, imports of foreign cotton yarn and cloth into Bengal had fallen by 25 and 40 per cent respectively. With the Extremists riding a wave of popular fervour, the Moderates were thrown on to the back foot, and despite engineering the election of the respected Dadabhai Naoroji as president, were unable to prevent the 1906 Calcutta Congress session from endorsing the New Party platform, *swaraj* and all.

Alarmed that their longstanding grip on the Congress appeared to be weakening, the Moderates clung to the hope that the new Liberal government in London would come to their rescue with a further substantial instalment of constitutional reform. In the meantime, they intrigued furiously to turn the tables on their opponents by the time of the next annual session, contriving to change the venue from Nagpur, a stronghold of Tilak, to Surat, a smaller, sleepier town on the west coast, and again prevailing on the local organising committee to nominate one of their own, Rash Behari Bose, as president. They may also have taken other precautions, too, such as stacking the key opening meeting with supporters specially trucked in from Bombay, though the evidence on this point is unclear. At any rate, when the proceedings at Surat got underway, the New Party found themselves out-manoeuvred and out-muscled. As Tilak tried to make himself heard from the platform, a shoe was thrown. The meeting degenerated into a chaos of scuffles and shouting-matches. Taking advantage of the confusion, the Moderates and their supporters reconvened the session in another part of town and pushed through a resolution binding all

Congressmen to pledge themselves to work by constitutional means towards the goal of Indian self-government within the British Empire.

Stunned by this machiavellian coup, the Extremists slunk home in total disarray, and over the next few years, most of their leaders went into voluntary or mandatory retirement: Aurobindo to the seclusion of a Pondicherry ashram; Lajpat Rai to the United States; Bipin Chandra Pal to London; Tilak to a Rangoon jail, courtesy of a six-year sentence imposed on him in 1908 for sedition. In their absence, the Moderates further consolidated their position, buoyed by the Morley–Minto reforms of 1909 and by the government's decision, in 1911, to reverse the partition of Bengal. No one could have guessed that the Moderate era had already passed its peak, and that within a decade the Congress organisation would be firmly in the grip of revolutionaries.

THE COMING OF THE MAHATMA

The outbreak of the First World War, triggered, ironically, by the over-zealous patriotism of another group of nationalists in the Balkans, had profound and far-reaching implications for India. Some of these, such as the financial burden imposed by India's contribution of men and money to the Allied cause, the political expectations aroused by the Allied war-aims, and the disorientating effect of foreign military service on hundreds of thousands of Indian volunteers, have already been mentioned. Others included grave shortages of basic commodities such as kerosene, soaring inflation, which generated windfall profits for the mercantile community but severely stretched the budgets of average consumers, and the conflict of loyalties created for Indian Sunni Muslims by the decision of their titular head (or Khalif), the Sultan of Turkey, to enter the war on the side of Germany and Austria-Hungary. The hopes, the hardships and the excitements of the war gave a heightened impetus to Indian nationalist politics. Even veterans like Surendranath Banerjea were galvanised into renewed action. Moreover, as the war crisis deepened, the nationalist movement itself underwent a remarkable transformation. As noted above, Gokhale and Mehta both died, prematurely, in 1915. This opened the way for the emergence of alternative leaders, notably Tilak, returned from Burma, Annie Besant, an English Theosophist who had taken up the national cause after receiving a psychic message from a spiritual being she identified as the '*mahatma*' ('great soul') Koot Hoomi, and a seasoned, but as yet little known, political worker from South Africa, M.K. Gandhi. What is more, Tilak and Besant quickly signalled that they intended to provide an alternative style of leadership. In 1916, the two, separately, launched Home Rule Leagues, modelled disturbingly (for the British) on the Irish Sinn Fein, and over the next two years they actively canvassed for members in a way the old Congress had never done. By 1918 the two Leagues together had nearly 60,000 paid-up cadres, a tribute both to the power of the Tilak name and to Besant's effective use of the Theosophical Society's extensive branch network to mobilise Madras, which had hitherto been a somewhat backward province politically. However, neither Tilak, for reasons of declining health, nor Besant, because she was in the last resort a white woman with residual racial ties to the Empire that she could never completely shake off, were able to sustain this momentum into the post-war era. Tilak died in 1920; shortly afterwards Annie fell out with the Congress and retired to a life of spirituality.

This left Gandhi to occupy the breach. By 1920 he had taken full command of the Congress and had become the leading spokesman for the independence movement. The latter role, at least, he never relinquished. What talents and circumstances made possible the achievement of this Gandhian hegemony?

When Gandhi returned to the land of his birth in 1915 after twenty years in South Africa, fighting for the rights of Indians there, he was already a mature politician with a comprehensive vision of the ideal Indian society and a plan for achieving it. His starting point, like Vivekananda's, was that Western technology had failed to add significantly to the sum of human happiness and, indeed, had enslaved men and women to the service of the machine [*Doc. 17*]. People were much happier, Gandhi believed, when they lived simply, in small communities, and provided for their own needs, for example by spinning and weaving their own garments. Freedom, he hoped, would be accompanied by the dismantling of the mega-state and a return to the self-sufficient village of the past. Of course, the idea was impractical and was privately scorned by many of his nationalist colleagues, but it identified him as an authentic Indian with a genuine affection for the material culture of the masses. Moreover, whereas Tilak's populism had never carried over into his personal life, Gandhi increasingly affected a peasant lifestyle. Always a vegetarian, he ate, as time went by, more and more frugally. He took to hand-spinning. After returning to India he discarded coat and trousers for the simple *dhoti* (loin-cloth) worn by men of the villages. Where possible, he walked. The Indian masses opened their hearts to Gandhi because, unlike other Indian politicians, he looked and acted like one of themselves. Nevertheless, what mattered most to Gandhi was the inner person, not the outer shell. And in this respect his philosophy was simple but uncompromising. The good man or woman had, first, to be truthful. 'I worship God', he wrote, 'as Truth only' [38 *p. 204*]. Secondly, he or she had to be absolutely non-violent. This strong moral stand gave Gandhi's political actions a stamp of integrity, even something of a 'saintly' quality. And the latter was reinforced by his personal austerity, by his preference for living communally in *ashrams*, surrounded by disciples pledged to a life of disinterested public service, and by his decision to 'purify' himself by renouncing sex, an act which most Indians, drawing on traditional beliefs linking the emission of semen with loss of strength, interpreted as a sign of power. The title given him in 1920, Mahatma, was well deserved.

But the Mahatma did not just offer a prescription for moral living; he offered a strategy for winning freedom from British rule. The strategy was called *satyagraha*, or truth-force. Like many of Gandhi's ideas, *satyagraha* owed something to a variety of literary sources. In this case, the main influences were the writings of the Russian Leo Tolstoy and the American Henry Thoreau about 'civil disobedience', which argued that arbitrary laws could be defeated if enough people concerted together peacefully to resist them. This theory appealed to Gandhi both because it was in consonance with his own deeply-held beliefs, and because passive resistance seemed the only recourse for India given the enormous disparity in power between the government and its subjects. But in adapting the notion of civil disobedience to India's situation, Gandhi also added something of his own, namely the power of truth to resolve conflict. He believed that if the resister behaved with absolute honesty, hiding nothing, and made it clear to his adversary that he was ready to suffer cheerfully whatever punishment came his way, sooner or later the adversary's conscience would be pricked. Again, this radical and idealistic notion did not commend itself, initially at least, to many of Gandhi's colleagues, who found it difficult to imagine any of the sun-dried British bureaucrats of their acquaintance undergoing a moral conversion. Yet *satyagraha* was probably the perfect implement of mass resistance in the circumstances of early twentieth-century India. Time and again, the British would be shamed into giving ground by the Mahatma's palpable decency [*Doc. 18*].

Indeed, in this, as in other respects, Gandhi showed very shrewd political judgement. To be sure, it would be wrong to say that he 'used' religion for political ends, as some have suggested. Religious values were always at the forefront of his decision-making. However, in so far as his moral philosophy and social vision for India required him to participate in the political process, he did so with great polish and perspicacity. One example of this was Gandhi's cautious initial approach to the Congress. When he returned to India, he deliberately stayed in the background for a year, observing the dynamics of the national movement. His humility eased the suspicions of the established leaders that he was planning to usurp their position. Then, when he did move, he kept his first political forays small-scale and manageable, as when in 1917 he intervened to help the rack-rented indigo cultivators of Champaran district in north Bihar. Through these successful interventions, he enhanced his reputation as a politician who could deliver on his promises. Another example was the way Gandhi used the opportunities afforded him during 1917–18 to develop useful professional relationships with some rising regional leaders such as the Bihari lawyer Rajendra Prasad, the mayor of Ahmedabad Vallabhbhai Patel, the Madrasi Brahmin C. Rajagopalachari, and the young Jawaharlal Nehru, who seems to have found in the Mahatma the approachable father he lacked in Motilal (and perhaps, also, an antidote to his sense of cultural alienation). Today we would call this networking. Yet a third intervention was the focused way Gandhi went after the Muslims and the business community, two strategically important but hitherto neglected Indian constituencies. He pursued the former by shamelessly exploiting Muslim anxiety over the security of Islamic holy places 'liberated' by Allied forces in the Middle East and the fate of the Khalif should Turkey lose the war. And he made the most of his Gujarati background and connections (he was a member of the *bania*, or merchant caste, born in Porbandar) in shaping his pitch to the Ahmedabad business community. Again, it is a measure of the Mahatma's astuteness that these two groups richly repaid his attentions, the Muslims by backing his takeover of the Congress in 1920, and the Gujarati industrialists by bankrolling the subsequent Non-Cooperation campaign.

However we should not assume that Gandhi returned to India bent on destroying the Raj. In 1915 he gracefully accepted the Kaiser-i-Hind medal awarded in recognition of his services to the Indian community in South Africa, and a major theme of his political speeches during that year was India's duty to do its bit for the Empire in the war. As late as 1918, he professed his admiration for British institutions and conventions of fair play. What converted him was the government's cynical betrayal of this noble heritage once the war had been won. First, on the strength of the report from a committee on 'sedition' headed by Justice S.A.T. Rowlatt, New Delhi introduced a bill to prolong indefinitely the life of the draconian regulations introduced to crush wartime dissent. Then came General Dyer's crime at Amritsar, rendered infinitely more repugnant in Gandhi's eyes by the tacit endorsement of his action by a large section of English opinion. This was followed, thirdly, by the news from the Peace Conference that Turkey was to be saddled with a huge war indemnity and stripped of its colonial territories, an outcome that confirmed the Muslims' worst fears of British duplicity. By 1920 Gandhi's faith in the British Empire had been 'shattered'. Moreover, he believed that in the light of the Rowlatt, Punjab and Khilafat 'wrongs', Britain no longer enjoyed any moral right to rule India, or to claim the allegiance of its 300 million subjects. In a letter to the viceroy he announced that he was starting a campaign of 'non-cooperation' with the object of bringing down the Raj. The campaign would begin, he advised, with a general boycott of British goods, and of government schools, colleges, law courts and legislatures [*Doc. 19*].

NON-COOPERATION AND AFTER

Gandhi's expectation was that the Raj would 'wither away' within the year. It didn't. One reason was the Mahatma's refusal to compromise his principles for political gain. Right from the beginning he was terrified of the prospect of the movement falling into the hands of the 'mob' and being tainted by mob violence. Therefore, in the first instance, he deliberately targeted arenas of government (such as civil justice) where Indian non-participation was unlikely to provoke a showdown with the police. Full-scale non-cooperation, inclusive of such areas of government as taxation and the administrative services – the areas, in other words, really vital to the functioning of the Raj – was only scheduled to kick in later, after the people had had a chance to show their mettle. And this stage was never reached. In February 1922, just as the first round of full civil disobedience was about to start (with a tax strike in the Bardoli subdivision of Gujarat), Gandhi learned that Congress workers in a village in Gorakhpur, Chauri Chaura, had torched a police station, incinerating twenty-two constables. To the amazement of most of his colleagues, he at once suspended the entire movement [*Doc. 20*]. Shortly afterwards he himself was arrested, tried and sentenced to six years in jail. But the main reason non-cooperation failed to achieve its major objective was that not enough Indians responded to the Mahatma's call. Many students, to be sure, took the opportunity to dodge examinations. And a large majority of qualified voters declined to exercise their franchise in the 1920 elections: up to 90 per cent in a few areas. But although 200 lawyers stopped work, the courts continued to function, and hardly any ranking public servants resigned their posts.

The struggle for freedom in South Asia has been likened to a Gramscian war of position for hegemony over the hearts and minds of the Indian people [39 *pp. 507–8*]. As we have seen, the strongest pillar of the Raj was the fact that, ultimately, its rule was accepted and tolerated by the majority. That being so, the essential task of the freedom movement was to wrest control of the peoples' allegiance from the Raj. From this perspective, the 'surrender' of 1922 looks less like a crushing defeat (which is, of course, how it was portrayed by the British), and more like a tactical withdrawal (which is how Gandhi saw it). Long before the murder of the policemen at Chauri Chaura it had become very clear to the Mahatma that, first, for whatever reason, most Indians were not yet prepared to sacrifice their comforts and their careers for the national cause; secondly, that many of those who were so prepared lacked the mental discipline to confront the Raj non-violently. Accepting that he had badly miscalculated, in 1922 Gandhi mixed pragmatism with high-mindedness and called a halt while the movement's structure and morale remained intact. Although some were bemused and offended by the apparent whimsicality of Gandhi's decision, it was the right one in the circumstances and ensured that the Congress lived to fight another day.

As it was, the Congress emerged from the experience of Non-Cooperation greatly strengthened. Some older groups of supporters had dropped off in 1920, alienated by the organisation's shift from pressure-group politics to open agitation; others, notably the Khilafatist Muslims, left in 1922, exasperated by what they saw as a failure of nerve on the part of the Mahatma. But these losses were offset by big gains among other classes and in formerly backward regions. During Non-Cooperation, total Congress membership increased dramatically from under 100,000 to a peak of around two million at the end of 1921; many of these new supporters came from affluent sections of the peasantry and from the commercial castes, but they also included railway workers and mill-hands, and in some regions a sprinkling of poor tenant-farmers, who by this time had begun to organise themselves locally into *kisan sabhas* (peasant leagues). Before 1920 Congress had been an elite body, dominated by the professional middle classes from the presidencies of Bengal and Bombay; after 1920 it became a mass organisation, preponderantly a vehicle of the urban commercial classes and the rich peasants of Gujarat, the Andhra region of Madras, the United Provinces (UP) and Bihar. These new recruits represented a sizeable dent in the Raj's political constituency. Another gain was the administrative restructuring which Non-Cooperation forced on the Congress. The organisation that Gandhi inherited in 1920 consisted of three administrative levels: a district branch level; a provincial committee level; and an all-India level made up of the general secretary and an All-India Congress Committee (AICC). In 1920 the AICC was democratised: membership was raised from 161 to 350; seats were re-allocated among the regions on a population basis, which greatly reduced the numerical influence on decision-making of Bengal and Bombay; and strenuous efforts were made to recruit from special-interest constituencies such as trade unions and women. At the same time, about 100 additional district branches were formed, and several hundred more at village level, which further reinforced Congress' penetration of the countryside, while a new peak policy and administrative cell was tacked on to the existing structure – the Congress Working Committee (CWC). As well as adding to the reach and efficiency of the organisation, these changes added immensely to its stature, transforming it from a lobby-group into something akin to an Indian parliament. As Gandhi remarked pointedly, 'The Working Committee is to the Congress what a Cabinet is to Parliament' [77 *p. 415*]. Gandhi's idea was that the Congress should slowly evolve into an alternative Raj, in preparation for the day when it would be required to take over the governance of the subcontinent.

Moreover, the cessation of Non-Cooperation allowed the Congress to add other strings to its political bow. In 1923 the AICC resolved to lift the ban on Congressmen standing for election, and a number took the opportunity to contest the polls held in that year, generally successfully. The strategy was that the party would engage in 'responsive non-cooperation' from within the councils, thereby wrecking the Montford reforms. In fact, the presence of the Congress legislators helped to legitimate the new constitution. But, paradoxically, it also helped restore the image of the Congress in the eyes of the 'respectable' upper-middle class, which had never felt comfortable with Gandhian populism. Meanwhile, at the direction of the Mahatma himself, who remained sceptical of the utility of constitutional politics, Congress pressed on with the other side of its agitational agenda, namely nation-building. When he got out of jail in 1924, Gandhi set up the all-Indian Spinners' Association to spread the cause of hand-spinning and weaving and more generally of economic self-reliance. At the same time he pushed Congress into supporting programmes to spread mass literacy and improve village sanitation. Last but not least, he began to campaign vigorously for the ending of the stigma of untouchability which for centuries had prevented the lowest castes from worshipping in temples, using village wells, and in some areas even approaching within eyeshot of high-caste persons. Although his interventions in the latter sphere, especially, were not universally welcomed – for instance, the self-proclaimed untouchable leader B.R. Ambedkar found his emphasis on promoting reconciliation within the framework of the caste system insulting – overall this programme of 'constructive work' considerably raised the reputation of the Congress as a 'moral' organisation dedicated to the national good.

Some Congressmen would probably have been happy to prolong this relatively undemanding regime of responsive non-cooperation and constructive work indefinitely; others, hungry for action, soon grew restless. Paramount among the latter were a group whom Gandhi was later to call 'the young hooligans': Jawaharlal Nehru, Jayaprakash Narayan and Subhas Chandra Bose. All three men were attracted to socialism (which equated to hooliganism in the Mahatma's conservative eyes). Socialist rhetoric, in turn, informed their anti-imperialism. From the mid-1920s, Nehru, Narayan and Bose lobbied furiously on the AICC and in the CWC for a renewed push for freedom [*Doc. 21*].

Initially, Gandhi sided with other conservatives in the high command to resist this demand, thinking the Congress was not yet ready to resume open agitation. But the march of events – the appointment of the all-British Simon Commission, the death of revered nationalist Lajpat Rai in an anti-Simon demonstration in 1928 and a sudden collapse of agricultural prices – forced his hand. Fearful lest the mounting national anger and distress spilled over into violent revolt, Gandhi persuaded the Calcutta Congress session of 1928 to give the British a year to grant India Dominion Status. In return for this concession he promised the militants that he would launch a new campaign of civil disobedience if the government failed to deliver. As we have seen, the government tried to head off this looming confrontation with the Irwin Declaration of October 1929. But the Congress by this stage had had its fill of open-ended British promises. At the Lahore annual session of December 1929, the party authorised the CWC to launch a campaign of mass protest, law-breaking and non-payment of taxes under Gandhi's direction. On 26 January 1930 (still observed as India's national day) huge crowds gathered in city and village to affirm their support for that stand. Still hoping, perhaps, to find a way out that did not involve the risky path of confrontation, on 31 January Gandhi wrote to Irwin with a list of demands. Significantly, they did not include the granting of *purna swaraj* (full independence), which struck some Congress workers as a back-down. However, the latter underestimated the shrewdness of the Mahatma's strategy. The ultimatum's emphasis on bread-and-butter issues, such as the pernicious salt tax, made the Congress position look reasonable in the eyes of the world and especially in American opinion, which had begun to take an interest in the Indian struggle. Also, it gave Gandhi a platform from which to launch civil disobedience on his own terms. When, as expected, Irwin rejected the proferred olive branch, the Mahatma wrote a second letter to Irwin informing the viceroy that he and seventy other members of his Ahmedabad *ashram* planned to walk to the coastal town of Dandi and, once there, to break the law by picking up duty-free salt.

With this symbolic act of civil disobedience on the Arabian seashore, Congress began its second campaign to topple the Raj. Lasting, in total, over four years, the Civil Disobedience Movement was undoubtedly a much more titanic event than its predecessor. It was substantially bigger, very much more intense, and affected far more of the subcontinent. Yet in one respect it compared unfavourably with the former movement. This time around there was little participation from Muslims. Explaining this important shift in national allegience is the task of the next chapter.

CHAPTER FOUR

MUSLIM SEPARATISM

THE NUMBERS GAME

Indian Muslims in the late nineteenth century suffered collectively from two disadvantages. The first, already noted, was their backwardness. Having taken to the new education more slowly and reluctantly than their Hindu equivalents, Muslim elites in north India found themselves increasingly muscled out of lucrative and influential bureaucratic jobs by clever immigrant Kayasthas and Brahmins from Bengal. It remained to be seen whether Sir Saiyyid Ahmad Khan's MAO College, which was funded to cater for only 100 or so boarding and day students at any one time, had the capacity to turn this alarming situation around.

The second was their numbers. The census of 1881 showed Muslims to be just under 20 per cent of the Indian population: more numerous than earlier guesstimates had predicted, but still a long way short of the biggest community, the Hindus, recorded as comprising almost three-quarters of the population. Provincially, the picture was more diverse but, once again, the bottom line was that Muslims were almost everywhere a minority: about 30 per cent in Bengal, just 6 per cent in Madras, barely 3 per cent in the Central Provinces and, more importantly, only about 14 per cent in the North-Western Provinces and Oudh (UP), the traditional heartland of Muslim power. Formerly this had not been a problem because the Raj had been an autocratic government. So long as all important governing decisions are made *for* a people rather than *by* them, numbers do not count for much politically. But once the British began tentatively to move towards setting up a representative system, the Muslims' lack of numbers became a potential hazard. If people chose to cast their votes along communal lines, Muslim candidates would stand very little chance, except perhaps in the Punjab and Bengal, of being elected. But there was another dimension too. Democratic politics opened up the prospect of the unlettered masses getting power. This prospect greatly frightened the gentrified Muslim leadership centred on Aligarh. 'Men of good family', Sir Saiyyid explained to a British friend, 'would never like to trust their lives and property to people of low rank' [57 *p. 61*].

Right from the start, therefore, Muslim elites (with the surreptitious backing of some conservative British officials), strenuously opposed the extension of the democratic principle in India. And since the Congress was a strong advocate of constitutional reform, they were drawn into opposing Congress too. Sir Saiyyid, the most rabid advocate of the anti-Congress position, ridiculed the organisation as a vehicle of effeminate Bengalis, and warned his fellow Muslims that if they associated with the organisation, they would be forced to 'lick Bengali shoes' [*Doc. 22*]. As a consequence of this propaganda, Muslim participation in the Congress, initially quite robust at around 16 per cent, dropped off dramatically in the 1890s. The Poona session of 1894 was attended by only twenty-five Muslims, as against 1,584 Hindus, while the Madras session of 1898 attracted just ten Muslim delegates out of 614. Although a few influential Muslims, such as Amir Ali of Calcutta and Badruddin Tyabji of Bombay, fought hard to stem the anti-nationalist tide, by the end of the century the Aligarh clique could claim, with some justification, that Congress was effectively a Hindu organisation.

However, while they were successful in their efforts to keep the Muslims out of Congress, Sir Saiyyid and his British friends were unable to stop or reverse the process of constitutional reform. Faced, as early as 1892, with the grim realisation that elections were likely to become a permanent feature of Indian political life, the Aligarh leadership looked for a way to keep the numerically disadvantaged Muslims in the game. Their best chance, they decided, was to make a claim for special consideration. This, in turn, required them to show that the Muslims constituted a separate community with unique needs and aspirations.

Earlier in his career, Sir Saiyyid had appeared to accept the idea of a single subcontinental nationality, on one occasion likening India to a beautiful woman, and the Hindus and Muslims to her two eyes. But by the 1880s this sentimental rhetoric had given way to a stridently separatist discourse focused on the pretensions of the Congress. 'I do not understand what the words "national Congress" mean', he wrote to Tyabji. 'Is it supposed to be that the different castes and creeds living in India belong to one nation, or can become a nation, and their aims and aspirations be one and the same? I think it is quite impossible and when it is impossible there can be no such thing as a national Congress' [57 *p. 61*]. Now, this was not an altogether unreasonable position. Hindus and Muslims are different in a number of ways. Hindus hold the cow sacred; Muslims eat beef. Hindu men generally go about clean-shaven; Muslim men often wear beards. Hindu women are permitted to appear in public with their faces uncovered; Muslim women generally are not. Hindus worship many gods; Muslims just one, Allah. And so on. However, in the context of late nineteenth-century India, the two communities also shared some things in common, such as the Hindustani (Urdu) language, and such differences as did exist were no greater than the differences between Hindus from different classes and regions. Ethnically, then, the case for a separate Muslim nation in India was, at best, moot. But nationhood was not yet the Muslims' goal. They shared the government's illusion of permanence. Expecting British rule to last into the foreseeable future, they canvassed the nationality argument merely to support their claim for special treatment. Moreover, when the Muslims in 1906 asked for, and received, permission to lay their case personally before the viceroy Lord Minto, they took the precaution of lacing the nationality argument with others of a more pragmatic nature. For instance, the delegation made much of the Muslims' aloofness from the *swadeshi* campaign raging in Bengal, and generally of their respectability and loyalty towards the Raj. The fact that the delegation was led by the Aga Khan, a titled Bombay magnate, lent weight to this claim.

At any rate, the pitch succeeded. Minto promised the delegation that the Muslims' 'rights and interests as a community' – his use of the term was, itself, an important concession – would be 'safeguarded by any administrative re-organization with which I am concerned' [68 *p. 278*]. Afterwards he wrote to Morley suggesting the inclusion in the reform package of a provision for separate Muslim electorates, as the best way of doing this. Gokhale's and the Congress's dismay when this undemocratic arrangement became law in 1909 has already been noted. Meanwhile, the Muslim leadership began to wonder, on the strength of its successful approach to the viceroy, whether Sir Saiyyid had been wise in ordering the Muslims in his circle to eschew agitational politics. Shortly before the Aga Khan's delegation was due to leave for Simla, news came through that the pro-Muslim governor of the new province of East Bengal, Sir Bampflyde Fuller, had resigned over the issue of the appropriateness of judicial reprisals against schoolboy demonstrators. Minto's acceptance of his resignation was widely interpreted, not least by the Muslims, as a cave-in to mob pressure. And there were other signs of communal discontent too. According to the secretary of the MAO College, Mohsin-ul-Mulk, some Aligarh graduates had begun to tire of Sir Saiyyid's servile brand of loyalism and were in danger of drifting into the nationalist camp [*Doc. 23*]. In December 1906 Muslim leaders met under the chairmanship of the Nawab of Dacca to consider the problem. They decided that the community needed a voice of its own, an organisation complementary to the 'Hindu' Congress. Thus was the All-India Muslim League born.

Pakistani historians see the formation of the League as a national milestone. After all, the League led the successful Pakistan struggle of the 1940s. But this interpretation fails to acknowledge the intervening vicissitudes experienced by that organisation. Several times, as we shall see, it came close to disintegrating. And its political orientation was by no means consistent throughout its history. For instance, while the League began life as an avowedly anti-Congress body, over the next decade it moved progressively towards the nationalist mainstream under the impetus of a Muslim 'Young Party' composed of Aligarh graduates and religious scholars connected to the traditionalist and vehemently anti-British seminary at Deoband in the United Provinces. In 1910 the Young Party prised control of the League away from Mohsin-ul-Mulk's group at Aligarh College, and moved its headquarters to Lucknow. From this base, they began discussing with Congress leaders the possibility of negotiating an agreed common platform of broad nationalist objectives. The outcome was the Congress–League Reform Scheme of 1916, colloquially known as the Lucknow Pact, which proposed an expansion of the legislative councils such as to create elected majorities, a substantial broadening of the franchise and electoral weightage (including separate electorates) for Muslims. Significantly, the League's chief spokesman in these talks was also an active member of the Congress, the Bombay-based Khoja barrister Muhammad Ali Jinnah. Jinnah was afterwards known with affection in both camps as 'the ambassador of unity'. Later in the war, Muslim politics was further radicalised by the Khilafat issue and by the government's heavy-handed repression of domestic dissent. In March 1919 joint Hindu–Muslim demonstrations against the Rowlatt Bills culminated in the Arya Samaj leader Swami Shraddhanand being invited to speak from the pulpit of the Jumma Masjid, Delhi's holiest Islamic shrine. The history of the League, and more generally of political Islam, at this time, is conspicuously bereft of the separatist tendencies that we associate with the Pakistan movement.

A stronger case can be made out for separate electorates. Although Muslims were permitted to vote also in the general constituencies, and often did so, the creation of special electorates in which only Muslims could vote gave an enormous filip to the notion that they comprised a distinct community. And every election after 1909 gave further substance to that perception. Every time a Muslim exercised his franchise in a reserved seat, he ritually affirmed his connections to other Muslims and his separateness from other Indians. Paradoxically, though, separate electorates did not, as expected, promote internal solidarity within the community. Elections are contests in which candidates sell themselves by demonstrating an identity of interest with the voters. What did the voters in these constituencies have in common? Obviously, their identity as Muslims. But appeals to communal solidarity were of limited value when one's opponents were also Muslims. Accordingly, candidates in these contests strove to prove they were 'better' Muslims than their rivals by spicing their speeches with quotations from the *Qur'an* and having their campaigns blessed by local religious leaders, such as the often-bigoted *mullahs*. In this way Muslim politics in colonial India at the local level came gradually to acquire a communal and Islamic character that sat uneasily with the sincerely professed secularism of all-India leaders such as Jinnah and Fazli Husain.

THE 'PARTING OF THE WAYS'

So far our analysis of the separatist tendency among Indian Muslims has been confined to the actions and reactions of elites. The argument offered in the preceding section was that certain privileged Muslim groups in north India pushed the notion of Muslim separateness as a defence against the threats posed to their social position by the introduction of representative government and competitive recruitment to the public service.

But this argument would be fraudulent as well as cynical if it did not take into consideration the larger arena of Hindu–Muslim relations. As we have seen, the two communities were divided by fundamental differences of belief, and while the hard edges of religious theory were often softened by syncretic practice (a tendency rooted in the fact that most Muslims in the subcontinent were descendants from Hindu converts), enough remained to provide lively ammunition for discord. One common irritant was the loud music favoured by Hindus as an aid to worship. Bells, gongs and cymbals are an intrinsic part of temple ritual, and no Hindu procession is complete without a band. Muslims, on the other hand, prefer to pray in silence. Sometimes Hindus deferred to this sensitivity by stopping their music during Muslim prayer times; sometimes they did not. The latter choice almost always resulted in physical violence. Festivals, too, often gave rise to physical clashes, in particular the noisesome Hindu Holi festival and the Muslim festival of Bakr'Id, at which animals, including cows, were ritually sacrificed. Of course these causes of friction were not new. They had been present for as long as Hindus and Muslims had lived together in South Asia. But from the late nineteenth century there was an increasing tendency on both sides for devotees to be less tolerant of each others' ritual needs and actively to seek out opportunities for confrontation, for instance, by deliberately routing their processions to inflict maximum disruption. One contributary factor to this mentality shift, perhaps, was the British government's well-intentioned policy of religious neutrality, which encouraged Indians of all faiths to think they had an absolute right to carry out their particular rites regardless of their impact on non-believers. (Until well into the twentieth century religious riots were much less frequent in the princely states, whose governments did not maintain a position of neutrality in matters of belief.) Another, clearly, was the aforementioned religious 'revival'. In the past Hinduism had tended to view all other religions with a haughty indifference. However revivalist organisations such as the Arya Samaj spurned this passive approach in favour of a militantly pro-active one. The Aryas openly criticised Islam (and for that matter, Christianity). They agitated for the 'protection' of cows, a move that brought them into direct conflict with Muslim butchers. They pursued converts, employing the Christian technique of baptism (*shuddhi*) to reclaim Hindus 'lost' to Islam. Meanwhile, other Hindu militants, especially in the United Provinces, lobbied to have Urdu replaced by Hindi as the main language of administrative record. Unused to this aggressive, triumphalist brand of Hinduism, Muslims felt threatened. The fact that some of the loudest spokesmen for the Hindu cause and some of the biggest donors to the Arya Samaj and the cow protection movement came from the Hindu merchant and money-lending communities, the principal agents of lower-class Muslim economic dependency, reinforced this sense of insecurity.

Not surprisingly, they attempted to strike back. Muslims with money and education responded in kind, setting up organisations to counter the Hindu missionary push. One such society, established in Lahore in 1885, put much effort into housing and educating orphans 'so as to save them from falling into the hands of the followers of other religions' [38 *p. 157*]. Another, founded at Aligarh in 1894, campaigned for the preservation of Urdu. Still more important initiatives were launched in the early 1920s, notably the *tanzim* (organisation) and *tabligh* (education) movements which sought to consolidate the Muslim community by purifying Indian Islam of 'heretical' (that is to say, syncretic) practices. Poor Muslims, meanwhile, lacking other weapons, responded with violence. Everywhere that the Samaj and the Cow Protection Society opened branches, communal riots proliferated, peaking in the bloody 'cow' riots of 1893 [*Doc. 24*]. Yet, far from being intimidated, Hindu revivalists perversely welcomed these encounters as opportunities to get even with an old foe. In the aftermath of the 1893 riots Pandit Bishan Narayan Dhar of Lucknow observed: '[they] will go far to bind the Hindu community together more firmly than ever. It has always been the tendency of persecution to create a spirit of fierce resistance and unity in the persecuted' [54 *p. 334*].

And the process did not stop there. Each year brought new riots, and each new riot left an additional burden of death and recrimination. By the end of the century, Hindu–Muslim relations had become so soured by this deadly roundabout of blood-letting, grief and revenge that it would have taken a mighty concerted effort by the leaders of the two communities to repair the breach. This effort was never forthcoming.

The nearest approximation came in the latter stages of the war, when Gandhi won over many Muslim hearts by taking up the cause of the Khalif and the Islamic holy places. But that – always flimsy – foundation for *rapprochement* was swept away by the suspension of the Non-Cooperation campaign and the republican Turkish government's abolition of the Khilafat two years later. Without an obvious point of political contact, the two

communities lapsed back into the cheap politics of antagonism. Congressmen were already regretting the generous electoral deal awarded Muslims
under the Lucknow Pact of 1916. Extended to local government in 1922,
the arrangement had allowed Muslims to capture over one-third of district
board seats in the United Provinces, more than twice what they would have
secured under a system of joint electorates. When C.R. Das in 1923 negotiated a pact for Hindu–Muslim electoral cooperation in Bengal, he was
repudiated by the AICC. Not surprisingly, the League took this as a signal
that all deals were now off. Political appeals to communal values were
encouraged, too, by the 1919 constitutional reforms, which confronted
politicians with the challenge of winning over an electorate too numerous
to be manipulated by the old mechanisms of personal patronage. Particularly in the Punjab, local Hindu Sabhas had been a feature of the
political landscape since the 1890s, and in 1915 UP Congressman Pandit
Mohan Malaviya had tried unsuccessfully to weld these into a political
party, the Hindu Mahasabha. Significantly, Malaviya chose this time to
revive his scheme. In 1926 the Mahasabha contested its first election.

But for a long time the Mahasabha remained too weak to cause much
real concern to the Muslims. Congress was quite another matter. Officially,
Congress remained a secular party dedicated to the goal of Hindu–Muslim
unity. Nevertheless, much to the chagrin of the party's leaders, some
Congress candidates insisted on playing the Hindu card at the polls in order
to checkmate the potential appeal of the Mahasabha. Moreover, even as the
party professed its secularism, its rhetoric and style sent a rather different
message. We have already remarked on the allusions to Hinduism contained
in the party anthem *Bande Mataram* and on the *Ramayana* symbolism in
Gandhi's political discourse. Muslims were also repelled by Gandhi's asceti-
cism, by the superstitious reverence in which he was held by many of his
followers, and by the Mahatma's insistence that all Congress party members should devote a part of their day to spinning (which struck them as an
unmanly activity). Ironically, one of the Muslims who left Congress at this
time specifically because of Gandhi's hegemony over the party was the
Ambassador of Unity, Muhammad Ali Jinnah, a dedicated secularist!

Nevertheless Jinnah continued to try, in the face of considerable
opposition within his own ranks and against a background of rapidly
escalating communal violence, to bring Congress and the League together
as a first step towards resolving the communal problem. In 1927 he
managed to persuade the League to agree to a bold offer: the discontin-
uance of separate electorates in return for a guaranteed one-third share of
seats in the Central Legislative Assembly and the separation of Sind from
Bombay to create a new Muslim-majority province. But the Congress
dismissed the offer as a desperate one made out of weakness. Nor did it
give much more than a second glance to the League's less generous offer of

1929, based on a 14-point compromise plan drafted by Jinnah [*Doc. 25*].
So discouraged was Jinnah by these rebuffs that he temporarily retired from
politics to practise law at the English bar.

Was this, as Jinnah averred at the time, the 'parting of the ways' for
India's Hindus and Muslims? In some ways the comment was prophetic.
The Muslim League and the Indian National Congress would continue to
negotiate right down to the eve of independence in 1947, but Congress
would never receive a better offer for an amicable political settlement. Nor
would there ever be another Lucknow-style *rapprochement*. After 1929 the
two parties would never again work together for the national good. Yet in
other ways, perhaps, the forecast was premature. For one thing, Jinnah
himself was still prepared to do deals. On his return to India in 1936, he
resumed the League leadership, this time as its permanent president, and
one of his first tasks in this new role was to oversee the League's campaign
for the first round of provincial elections under the revamped 1935
constitution. To the annoyance of some Muslim hardliners, he ran on a
platform of broad national issues and offered only moderate criticism of the
Congress in his campaign speeches. Then, following the predictable Congress victory, Jinnah approached Nehru with the suggestion that the two
parties share ministerial power in the interests of communal harmony. For
another thing, as its showing at the 1936 polls demonstrated, the League
did not at this stage speak for even the majority of Indian Muslims. Too
financially strapped to contest in other than Muslim constituencies, the
League won only 109 of these (out of a possible 482). More embarrassingly
still, the party received just 5 per cent of the total Muslim vote. Ironically,
its strongest showing was in the Muslim minority provinces, especially the
United Provinces, where it could never expect to govern. If the League at
this time was moving towards a position of separatism, which is dubious,
other Muslim or dominantly Muslim parties, such as the aptly-named
Unionist Party of the Punjab (and for that matter most of the country's
Islamic leadership, the *ulema*) were still committed to the ideal of a united
India.

HOMELANDS

Given that most Indian Muslims now believed they belonged to a distinct
and separate community, what were their options? The most straight-
forward option, and the one that Jinnah and his chief lieutenant, Liaquat
Ali Khan, both personally preferred (Jinnah, perhaps, because he still
fondly imagined himself as the prime minister of a future independent
India), was to stick to the policy the League had followed since 1909, which
was to seek constitutional protection for Muslims by way of weightage,
reserved seats and (eventually) reserved ministerial places. The other option,

at once much riskier and more daring, was to attempt to create a separate Muslim homeland somewhere in the subcontinent.

The latter was a logical extension of Sir Saiyyid Ahmad Khan's theory of Muslim nationality. As we have seen, it was accepted wisdom in the early twentieth century that nations had a right of self-determination, and of course Congress had long been advancing that claim on India's behalf. But it took another fifty years for Muslims to begin seriously to explore the political ramifications of Sir Saiyyid's vision: until 1930 in fact. And their initial attempts to give it concrete form were quite modest. The first substantial proposal for an Indian Muslim homeland is generally credited to the Urdu poet and philosopher Sir Muhammad Iqbal. However, Iqbal merely suggested that he would 'like to see the Punjab, North-West Frontier Province (NWFP), Sind and Baluchistan amalgamated into a single state'. Note that there is no mention here of Kashmir or Bengal, both Muslim-majority areas, or indeed of Muslim nationality. Nevertheless Iqbal's speech struck a chord with many educated Muslims, and in 1934 one of these, Chaudhri Rahmat Ali, a young man from a well-to-do Punjabi family doing postgraduate work at Cambridge University, published an elaboration of Iqbal's scheme. Rahmat Ali's scheme was territorially more ambitious, embracing as it did the princely state of Kashmir. It was also more fully worked out in terms of the governing structure. Most importantly of all, his Muslim state had a name, Pakistan. It was a clever choice, being at once an acronym ('P' stood for Punjab, 'A' for Afghan, which designated the NWFP, 'K' for Kashmir, 'S' for Sind, and 'TAN' for Baluchistan) and a pun (Pakistan in Urdu means land of the pure). But while Rahmat Ali's scheme was widely and often approvingly discussed by the Muslim laity, it was disdainfully ignored by the Muslim political leadership. Jinnah refused even to meet with its author. The numerous alternative Muslim homeland schemes dreamed up over the next few years fared little better.

By the end of the decade, however, the League's high command had substantially modified its position on the homeland issue. Perhaps the major reason was Congress intransigence. It is easy to see why Congress after the 1936 elections declined to take up Jinnah's power-sharing offer. The two parties differed on many issues, especially land reform; the League was a communal party and the Congress ostensibly a secular one; holding comfortable majorities in six provinces, Congress did not need the League's support to form a government. Nevertheless, with the benefit of hindsight, one can see that this was a strategic mistake. Besides, the negotiations were badly handled by the Congress leadership. Instead of simply rejecting the offer, the Congress Working Committee came back with a counter-offer: that the League's legislators should resign and join the Congress. This was tantamount to telling the League to disband. Jinnah never forgot or forgave this humiliation. Then, in mid-1937, having for several months wrestled with its principles, Congress relented and took office in the provinces it had carried in the polls.

This was a moment Muslims had long feared; Congress rule, they had been told, would mean Hindu rule, discriminatory and oppressive. And in truth, some of the policies put into effect by the Congress provincial ministries were – if not actually discriminatory – certainly preferential to the Hindu majority. For instance, Muslims were justly angered by the additional emphasis on the Hindi language and on Hindu culture and history in Congress-run state schools. Soon anti-Congress sentiment (inflamed, to be sure, by clever League propaganda) was running high among aggrieved Muslim parents, among Muslim professionals who felt that their employment prospects had suffered, and among Muslim businessmen who had watched lucrative government contracts go to Hindu firms with Congress party connections. Widespread community relief, therefore, greeted the CWC's announcement in December 1939 that it had directed all the Congress ministries to resign in protest at the viceroy's decision to take India into the war without consulting public opinion. The League's leaders marked the day dramatically by offering up prayers thanking Allah for delivering India's Muslims 'from tyranny, oppression and injustice during the last two and a half years' [68 *p. 329*].

The other main factor was the lure of power. The massive INC mandate in the 1937 elections impressed the League's leadership, as it did the British, with the huge popularity of Congress throughout the greater part of India. Although Jinnah and possibly others would still have preferred to exercise supreme power as members of a unitary government, they now saw that option slipping away, probably beyond recall. The next best option for these ambitious men was to seek power within the smaller sphere of a separate Muslim state.

As early as 1938 a resolution in favour of the homeland option was carried at the annual conference of the Sind Muslim League. Seeing where the momentum lay, the Council of the All-India League agreed to sponsor a similar resolution at the party's 1940 annual session, to be held at Lahore. It was passed by a huge majority. Jinnah's presidential speech supporting the resolution remains to this day the classic exposition of the 'two nation' theory on which Pakistan's existence ultimately rests.

Yet while it is often dubbed the 'Pakistan resolution', the formulation put to the party faithful at Lahore conspicuously avoided using the crucial P-word. Only years later did it come into common usage. Moreover, the resolution was only marginally less vague than Iqbal's. It talked simultaneously about 'geographically contiguous units', 'zones' and 'Independent States'. While nominating the Muslim-majority areas of eastern India as constituting one zone, its use of the plural suggested not one 'Pakistan' but two or perhaps even three such homelands. Although the term 'units' could

1. The collaboration of Indian elites was an important bulwark of empire in South Asia: the Lieutenant-Governor of the Punjab meeting representatives of the Indian aristocracy, Government House, Lahore, late nineteenth century.

2. A *zamindar*'s affluence – Raja Mullick's Palace, Chitpoor Road, Calcutta.

3. Protest in Bombay, 1930, against the importation of British goods. This protest was organised by Congress as part of the Civil Disobedience Movement. Police firing on demonstrators led to the killing of several young Congress supporters.

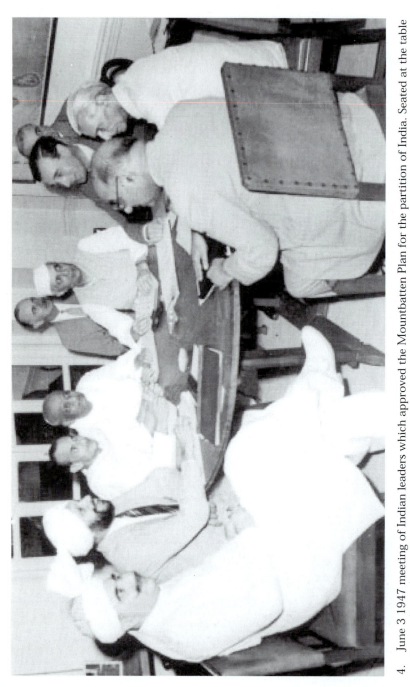

4. June 3 1947 meeting of Indian leaders which approved the Mountbatten Plan for the partition of India. Seated at the table are Balder Singh (second from left) representing the Sikhs, Vallabhbhai Patel and Jawaharlal Nehru from the Congress (fourth and fifth from left) and Muhammad Ali Jinnah representing the Muslim League (far right). Viceroy Lord Mountbatten is seated between Nehru and Jinnah.

be applied equally to princely states as well as provinces, the absence of any mention of Pakistan seemingly ruled out a claim to Kashmir, an interpretation which the League's subsequent demand for 'six provinces' (i.e., Sind, NWFP, Baluchistan, Punjab, Bengal and Assam) supports [*Doc. 26*].

Was a resolution framed in this open-ended manner intended to be taken seriously? Or was it merely a high-stakes bargaining chip to force the British and the Congress to concede the League's longstanding demand that Muslims be given a special constitutional status? Historians have argued this point for years, and the jury is still out. But there are some good reasons for thinking that the League, at least in 1940–41, was still keeping its options open. One, already mentioned, is the studied vagueness of the Lahore resolution. A second is the telling evidence gathered by the government's Reforms Commissioner, H.V. Hodson, during his provincial tour of 1941. Almost all the Muslim politicians Hodson spoke to assumed that Pakistan would be part of a larger all-Indian federation. A third is the bitter logic the homeland option posed for the majority of senior League leaders. As the Lahore resolution frankly recognised, any separate Muslim states would necessarily have to be situated in the north-west and north-east of the subcontinent. But from Mughal times the heartland of Muslim power in India had been the area around Delhi and Aligarh; even in the 1940s most of the League's high command came either from that region or, as in the case of Jinnah, from the Bombay presidency. If the Pakistan scheme ever came to fruition, Jinnah and the millions of other Muslims living in the minority provinces faced the dismal prospect of having to choose between permanent exile in a strange country, or permanent segregation as second-class citizens of 'Hindu' India. No wonder they hesitated.

CHAPTER FIVE

HANDING OVER

THE CATALYST OF WAR

The viceroy, Lord Linlithgow's, announcement in September 1939 that India was at war with Germany jolted the Indian people into acknowledging a reality that time had somewhat obscured: India was still an integral part of the British Empire. There had been, to be sure, some devolution of power. But even the reforms introduced under the Government of India Act of 1935, which conceded the substance of self-government at the provincial level, contained significant checks designed to protect and perpetuate a hard core of British control. These included, specifically, statutory provisions binding the Indian government to continue to pay interest to holders of railway stock and the pensions of retired ICS officers, and giving the viceroy and his governors the power to veto legislation repugnant to British interests, and, more generally, a franchise elaborately gerrymandered to favour the election to the federal legislature of princely, business, landlord and communal representatives at the expense of nationalists. While the British no longer deluded themselves that their rule in South Asia would be permanent, and while they no longer talked glibly in Curzonist tones of hanging around for centuries, the terms of the 1935 Act showed that they had no immediate plans to depart, either. Five years in the making, and the longest statute ever enacted by the Westminster parliament, the Act was no stop-gap transitional measure towards full independence. It represented the furthest point the British government and people were prepared to go down the devolutionary path. By what magic, then, did India gain her freedom barely a decade later?

As we have seen, the British position in the subcontinent was underpinned, in the first instance, by a combination of coercive power and administrative efficiency, but by the 1940s these vital props of the Raj were beginning to corrode. Thanks to the policy of Indianisation, by 1939 there were nearly as many Indians in the ICS as Europeans, and by 1947 Indians outnumbered Britishers by 614 to 587. Although the transition in the officer corps of the Indian Army was slower to begin, there, too, significant strides were made during the 1940s, the Indian element rising from 10 per cent in 1939 to 25 per cent by 1947.

Contrary to earlier British fears, Indianisation did not, in itself, impair the efficiency of the administration. On the other hand, it had the more serious effect for them of diluting the attachment of the Army and the civil bureaucracy to the imperial cause. Following the fall of Singapore in 1942, some 60,000 Indian troops became prisoners of war of the Japanese. Offered their freedom and the chance to help the Japanese 'liberate' India, many changed sides. In 1943 these patriotic defectors were organised into the Indian National Army (INA) by the former Congress nationalist Subhas Chandra Bose, who had fled Bengal in 1941 to join up with the Axis. Although the INA did little actual damage in the field, the fact that thousands of Indian soldiers had seen fit to renounce their oath of allegiance to the King-Emperor raised serious doubts about whether the military could continue to be relied on to enforce imperial authority. These doubts were confirmed when ratings of the Indian Navy based at Bombay and other western Indian ports mutinied in February 1946. Although the situation on the civil side never quite reached this dangerous pitch, there, also, signs of demoralisation began to surface from the early 1940s, particularly during the period of the 'Quit India' disturbances from August 1942 to mid-1943. The governor of Bihar, for instance, expressed alarm at the slack performance of his armed police: 'Their hearts', he reported, 'are not in the job' [38 *p. 315*].

Efficiency *was* undermined, though, by the unprecedented strain put on the Indian services by the demands of total war. Unlike the war of 1914–18, the Second World War was not geographically remote from the subcontinent. Shortly after Japan's entry on the Axis side in December 1941, Calcutta, Madras and other ports along the Bay of Bengal came under attack from ships and aircraft of Admiral Nagumo's Indian Ocean taskforce, precipitating a mass exodus of coastal-dwellers to the relative safety of the hinterland. Several months later Burma was overrun, and in 1944 Burmese-based Japanese forces, aided by Bose's Indian National Army, crossed the Assam border and penetrated Assam as far as Imphal. By 1941 India was already a vital conduit for military supplies to the Soviet Union. With the Japanese advance it became a crucial strongpoint and later a springboard for the Allied counter-offensive. These strategic needs demanded that India be organised for total war, and the task of overseeing this process fell basically to the members of the elite services. Even if it had remained at full strength, the ICS would probably have been hard pressed to cope, given that much of the work (for example, civil defence) lay outside its traditional fields of expertise. But during the war competing manpower needs prevented London from injecting new blood into the Service to replace the officers lost to retirement, sickness and secondment to military duties. The ICS men who were left struggled on heroically, but at the expense of their health and morale. The result, by 1945, as Sir Stafford Cripps admitted during his speech in the parliamentary debate on the bill for the transfer of power, was 'an obvious and inevitable weakening of the machinery of British control' [19 *p. 394*].

Meanwhile, the forces arrayed against the Raj grew steadily in size, effectiveness and hegemonic power. The nineteenth-century Congress had been purely a middle-class movement; by 1938 the party, by its own accounting, had $4\frac{1}{2}$ million paid-up members. In addition, millions more, who had reservations about joining an outwardly revolutionary organisation, supported Congress sentimentally and with their votes at elections. In the lead-up to the 1936 polls, Nehru alone addressed crowds totalling ten millions. In the election itself, Congress won 74 per cent of the vote in Madras, 63 per cent in Bihar and the Central Provinces, 60 per cent in Orissa and 59 per cent in the United Provinces, an astonishing result by modern democratic standards. After 1936 even the British were forced to concede that Congress had a mandate to rule. Moreover, Congress was not the Raj's only opponent. By the late 1930s the majority of India's industrial workers had been organised into unions, some of them linked to the Congress, others clandestinely to the outlawed Communist Party of India (CPI). For a long time the solidarity of the union movement was undermined by factional bickering, but in 1935, in response to a directive from the Comintern in Moscow, the Marxists agreed to join with their nationalist rivals in a 'united front' against imperialism. Meanwhile, in the countryside, the hardships of the depression, which saw hundreds of thousands of peasants threatened with eviction for non-payment of rents and taxes, sparked an upsurge of rural militancy which swelled the ranks of the *kisan sabha* movement. By 1938, the Bihar Sabha alone boasted 250,000 members.

But it was not only the Left that grew in stature during this period; the Hindu Right also consolidated its position. In 1925, at the urging of Hindu Mahasabha leader Dr B.S. Moonje, Maratha Brahmin K.B. Hedgewar established the Rashtriya Swayamsevak Sangh (Association of National Volunteers) (RSS) at Nagpur. The stated mission of the RSS was to defend Hindus and Hindu values. For the first decade of its life the new organisation remained, for the most part, confined to its native Central Provinces, but from the late 1930s it began to spread rapidly across north India. When M.S. Golwalkar, an unabashed admirer of Adolf Hitler, took over the leadership of the RSS in 1940, he assumed dictatorial control over 100,000 cadres trained to a high level of military-style discipline. Meanwhile the Mahasabha itself, which had been languishing, gained a new lease of life in 1937 with the accession of the charismatic V.D. Savarkar, another Maharashtrian Brahmin, to the party presidency.

Fortunately for the Raj, the country's burgeoning nationalist organisations – Congress, League, Mahasabha, Socialists, CPI – never managed to translate their common anti-imperialism into a unitary struggle for freedom, perhaps because they held very different conceptions of what a free India should look like. For instance, the Communists, having long posed as the staunchest of anti-imperialists, turned full circle following the Nazi invasion of the Soviet Union in 1941 and became, for the rest of the war, *de facto* supporters of the government. Nevertheless, by the 1930s even Congress acting alone had the capacity to shake the imperial structure. In the first Civil Disobedience Movement of 1930–31, several hundred thousand Congressmen courted arrest by taking part in illegal demonstrations, picketing, and deliberately breaking the law; some 60,000 went to jail. Another 14,000 *satyagrahis* were imprisoned during the 'Individual' Civil Disobedience Movement of 1940–41. Even these largely non-violent mass actions placed a severe strain on the government's resources. But the Congress did not always stop at peaceful protest. Increasingly, Congress leaders showed a readiness to experiment with more drastic forms of agitation such as withholding taxes, a mood encapsulated in Gandhi's slogan for the Quit India Movement of 1942, 'do or die'. Revolutionaries acting under the Congress banner went further. In 1930 Bengali extremists raided the Chittagong armoury and killed the District Magistrate of Midnapore; in 1932 Abdul Ghaffar Khan's Redshirts briefly seized control of Peshawar and set up a parallel government there; during the 1942 movement, which the government correctly categorised as a full-scale rebellion, Congress cadres murdered ninety-three policemen and blew up 208 police stations, 332 railway stations and 945 post offices. How much of a threat these violent actions posed can be gauged from the severity of the government's reaction to them, which included not merely mass arrests but punitive fines, the razing of whole villages, public floggings, machine-gunning of demonstrators from the air and, in 1942, the deployment of some fifty-seven battalions of regular troops on counter-insurgency duty.

Yet neither of these two great movements achieved their ultimate objective. The Raj outlasted them as it had Non-Cooperation earlier, assisted, particularly in the 1930–34 showdown, by the Congress right wing's continuing reluctance to loose the wrath of the mob against their enemy lest they inadvertently triggered a class war or, worse, a total collapse of law and order. Technically the British remained in control of the subcontinent right down to 1947. Were these struggles, then, in vain?

By no means. The Congress organisation gained enormous respect and prestige through its heroic tilts at the overwhelming power of the Raj. Likewise, the willingness of Congress leaders to suffer arrest and imprisonment (in some cases for years on end) for the national cause, added greatly to their personal aura as politicians. It was the party's (well-deserved) reputation for struggle and sacrifice that, more than anything else, carried it to impressive wins in the 1936 elections and in the post-war polls of 1945.

Moreover, while Congress's agitational movements failed physically to dislodge the British from the subcontinent, they gradually sapped the imperialists' strength and will to rule. Each British 'victory' was won at greater physical, mental and financial cost. Each time, the margin between survival and extinction became narrower. Although there was never a fourth agitational movement as such, the mass demonstrations of 1945–46, in the wake of the abortive trial of the INA leaders, gave the Raj a glimpse of what lay in store if Congress was pushed too far. Accordingly, British policy after 1945 became wholly defensive, driven, in viceroy Lord Wavell's words, by the necessity of staving off a further 'mass movement or revolution which it is in the power of Congress to start and which we are not certain that we can control' [60 *p. 428*]. Indeed, by 1946 Wavell had begun to plan for an evacuation in the event of his negotiations with the Congress breaking down – an act of realism for which he was unceremoniously sacked by his political masters in London. This end-game of empire showed, too, the finite limits of repression. Each time the British cracked down, they made more enemies. Every son lost to a British bullet or bayonet earned them the permanent hatred of another extended family. But it didn't need something as tragic as a death to convert someone from an onlooker into a Congress cadre. As the case of 'Hazari' shows, a few strokes of a police *lathi* (for the heinous crime of wearing a Gandhi cap!) could achieve the same result [*Doc. 27*].

But it was not just nationalist belligerency and its deleterious impact on the services that forced the British to quit. The decision to transfer power was influenced too by their reluctant acknowledgement that, in Macaulay-esque terms, their task in the subcontinent had been accomplished. Perhaps the first moment of truth in this regard was the comprehensive Congress triumph in the elections of 1936, which finally exploded the myth that the 'real Indians' were indifferent to the call of nationalism. However, the defining watershed in British attitudes took place during the following two and a half years of Congress provincial government. To the surprise and pleasure of the viceroy and his governors, and to the surprise and dismay of many on the Left, the Congress ministers proved reasonably efficient and prudent administrators. What is more, they showed no compunction about using the police in 'defence of life and property', in some occasions incarcerating their own nominal supporters. After 1939 the British could not seriously question the competence of Congress to rule in their stead. At the same time the friendly working relationships which most of the provincial governors managed to build up with their ministers helped break down mutual stereotypes. Working together, the British and the Congress leaders started thinking about each other as individuals, rather than simply as embodiments of 'fanaticism' or 'reaction'. Trust began to replace suspicion and blind hostility. Five years later, at the conclusion of the war, these mental re-adjustments helped the two sides reach a speedy and largely amicable settlement to the Indian problem on the basis of a grant of dominion status, something Congress had previously ruled out as falling short of true independence.

Wartime exigencies also forced the hand of the rulers. As in 1914–18, the feeding and equipping of the fighting men prevailed over the needs of civilians. By 1940 there was rampaging inflation and a serious shortage of essential commodities, especially food. The well off got by with the aid of the black market, but the rest of the population had to rely on what they were allocated by the authorities. Even when the procurement system functioned well, it sentenced people to dire hardship; by the end of the war the average weekly ration per person was about 1,200 calories, barely enough to sustain life. When, as in Bengal in 1943, it collapsed, the poor starved. The official estimate is that 1.5 million died in this last and greatest of Bengal famines, but nationalist sources put the toll at closer to three million. By any standards it was a disaster, and it did irreparable damage to the credibility of British rule. Meanwhile, and more specifically, the military threat posed by the rapid Japanese advance across Asia, coupled with police intelligence reports that showed that many Indians naively accepted Tokyo's assertion that the forces of the Rising Sun were coming to India solely to liberate it from the British imperial yoke [*Doc. 28*], compelled the British to revise completely their comfortable timetable for the gradual demission of power. On 11 March 1942, three days after the fall of Rangoon, wartime prime minister Churchill announced that he was sending the Lord Privy Seal, Sir Stafford Cripps, to India with an offer designed to break the political deadlock. The gist of the offer was that India would be granted dominion status immediately 'upon the cessation of hostilities'. Although Cripps's mission proved futile (as perhaps Churchill intended it should) – Congress did not think much of an offer which granted no substantial immediate relief and which was conditional on the very uncertain prospect of an Allied victory – it was difficult for the British, thereafter, to rescind it, particularly since Britain's partner and banker, the United States, had made plain its 'in principle' support for early Indian independence [*Doc. 29*]. Repeated references to colonial emancipation and national self-determination in Allied wartime propaganda statements hoisted the British even more securely on this ideological petard. Finally, thanks to the military agreement of 1938, which made the British exchequer responsible for meeting the cost of future Indian Army campaigns beyond the borders of the subcontinent, the United Kingdom ended the Second World War with a debt to India of £1,300 million, an amount equivalent to almost half the country's GNP. After 1945 (as a series of nervous submissions from the Treasury to Cabinet delicately pointed out), Britain's continued solvency hinged to a very large extent on the negotiation of a satisfactory political settlement with its Indian creditors. That meant, effectively, a settlement with the leaders of the Indian National Congress.

However, the logic of a prompt and friendly handing over of power was not just confined to the sphere of inter-government debt; it applied equally to all areas of the imperial connection with India – to trade, investment, regional defence and diplomacy. Once the British had committed themselves to granting independence to the subcontinent, it was in their long-term economic and political interest to ensure that they departed on good terms with their likely successors. Wavell grasped this as early as 1944 [*Doc. 30*]. So, even earlier, did the leaders of the opposition British Labour Party, who at a private meeting with Jawaharlal Nehru at Stafford Cripps's house in June 1938, undertook to pass a comprehensive independence bill as soon as they came to power. However, hopes of an early Labour election victory were dashed by the intervention of the war, and by the time the party found itself in a position, seven years later, to honour that promise, an additional factor had intruded into the equation: the Muslim factor. When the incoming Labour Ministry led by Clement Attlee sat down in May 1945 to decide on their policy towards India, the main question they had to resolve was not whether power ought to be transferred. They had already agreed that it should be. The question was rather, to whom?

TOWARDS PARTITION

When Mohammad Ali Jinnah took over the leadership of the All-India Muslim League in 1936 he inherited a party all but moribund: fragmented, demoralised and chronically short of funds. But over the next decade the League underwent a remarkable renaissance. It was this somewhat unlikely transformation that, more than anything else, made the establishment of Pakistan possible.

Undoubtedly, an important factor in the League's revival was the astute, visionary and at times ruthless leadership of Jinnah himself, who, in comparison to his Congress opposite numbers, had the further advantage of being virtually a one-man band. Learning from the party's abysmal showing in the 1937 elections, Jinnah set about rebuilding the League by reducing membership fees (to an affordable two annas), opening new branches and recruiting a crop of energetic and talented professionals, many of them graduates of Aligarh, to staff the party organisation. Within two years, these measures had swelled the League's membership at least tenfold, a good proportion of this growth occurring in regions where, hitherto, the League had been weak or non-existent, such as princely Rajputana and central India, and (importantly for future developments) Punjab. In turn, the League's evolution into a mass party made it a more saleable asset, allowing Jinnah to secure valuable financial backing from wealthy Muslim businessmen such as M.A.H. Ispahani, with whose assistance he acquired the newspaper *Dawn* to serve as a mouthpiece for Muslim opinion.

But the march of events during this decade also favoured the League. As we have seen, Congress provincial rule alienated many Muslims. This made them easy targets for Jinnah's recruiting drive. Secondly, the League benefited in several ways from the outbreak of war in 1939. While Congress took itself into dignified opposition in protest at the viceroy's decision to declare war without consulting Indian opinion, the League, which was ideologically far less anti-Fascist than the Congress, but whose supporters included many families with links to the Indian Army, announced that it would cooperate with the government in prosecuting the fight against the Axis. This pragmatic stance not only allowed the League to continue to function openly and legally during the war years, but also earned the party much imperial goodwill, evidenced in the viceroy's calling Jinnah in for summit talks at the end of 1939 (a gesture which was widely interpreted as giving official recognition to the League's claim to be regarded as the sole voice of Muslim India), in the comforting assurances embedded in the British government's August 1940 policy statement, and even more forthrightly in the Cripps' Offer, that power would not be transferred to any government or group whose authority was unacceptable to substantial elements of Indian society [*Doc. 31*], and in the favoured treatment received by the party in the provincial legislatures, which enabled it, in two cases, to form minority governments. Thirdly, the League profited from the heroic but foolhardy Congress rebellion of August 1942. Within twenty-four hours of the AICC passing the Quit India resolution, most of the party's top and middle-ranking leaders were in prison. The majority would remain there until 1945. Bereft of leadership, the Congress organisation decayed, opening up a power vacuum which the Mahasabha, the CPI and particularly the League hastened to fill.

One measure of the success of Jinnah's reinvigoration of the Muslim League was the party's showing in by-elections for the provincial assemblies. Between 1937 and 1945 it won fifty-five out of the seventy-seven by-elections for Muslim-reserved constituencies. By comparison, the next most successful Muslim party, the Punjab Unionist Party, won only nine, while Congress managed just four. However, the real turning point for the new Muslim League came with the general elections of December 1945 and January 1946. Despite facing a rejuvenated Congress, the League won four-fifths of all the Muslim-reserved seats on offer, enough to take the party into office in Sind and Bengal and within a whisker of provincial power in the Punjab. The result left no one, not least the British, in any doubt about where the locus of power within the Muslim community now lay.

Why did so many more Muslims cast their votes for the League in 1946 than in 1936? For one thing the party this time had a sure-fire vote-winning platform in its scheme for a Muslim homeland. Possibly because Pakistan remained such a very nebulous concept, it struck a chord with Muslims from a variety of social, sectarian and regional backgrounds. Muslim businessmen like Ispahani embraced it in the expectation that it would free them from the economic competition of Marwaris and Parsis. Indebted Punjabi Muslim landed families saw it as offering them a way out of their bondage to Hindu moneylenders. The religious-minded, including many members of the local Muslim clergy and the *pirs* who guarded the tombs of Muslim saints, saw in the scheme an opportunity to create an Islamic state governed by *shar'ia* law, an aspiration that the secularist League leadership hypocritically encouraged by remaining silent whenever it was canvassed. The Pakistan idea even gained a measure of support from Muslims living in the minority provinces, who naively assumed that the establishment of a Muslim state, incorporating within its boundaries millions of potential Hindu hostages, would render them less vunerable to majoritarian dis-crimination. For another thing, the League now possessed the resources to run a full-scale campaign. Through its daily national newspaper, *Dawn*, and an informal network of students from Aligarh, the party in 1946 was able to disseminate its message to a far wider audience than had been possible with the limited funds and contacts available ten years earlier. Finally, it would seem from anecdotal evidence that many people voted for the League out of deference to the wishes of the Islamic clergy, many of whom unblushingly used the pulpits of their mosques during the period of the election campaign to pump out pro-Pakistan propaganda. Indeed, if the testimony of one Punjab election agent is to be believed, there was common perception that anyone who did not cast his vote for the League 'would ... become [a] kaffir [heretic]' [76 *p. 124*].

In most respects, therefore, the League's success in the elections of 1945–46 can be interpreted as a clear Muslim mandate for Pakistan. Yet if this is correct, the outcome was ironic, because the League high command was still far from convinced that even a secular Pakistan, let alone the Islamic utopia envisaged by the clergy, would be in the best interests of Indian Muslims. Moreover, in the following months, the case for sticking with a united India became significantly stronger in the light of the recom-mendations of the three-member British Cabinet mission charged with the task of drawing up a detailed blueprint for the transfer of power. The Cabinet delegation not only mounted a powerful argument for holding that a sovereign Pakistan would not be economically viable, it also put up an ingenious plan for accommodating Muslim aspirations for a homeland within the framework of a unitary Indian state. Under the Cabinet Mission Scheme, the provinces would be 'free to form groups'. Three potential groups were envisaged, labelled A, B and C in the plan. Groups B and C were roughly equivalent to the western and eastern zones of the League's Pakistan. The groups would not be sovereign, but they would exercise many of the conventional powers of statehood. Only defence, communications, foreign relations and trade would lie with the centre.

A further consideration that weighed heavily with the League leadership was their awareness that the two-nation theory cut both ways. If history and culture demanded that Muslims and Hindus should live in separate states, partition logically could not follow the arbitrary boundaries of the British Indian provinces, for both Punjab and Bengal contained sizeable Hindu and Sikh minorities. Moreover, it was clear to the League leaders that the British and the Congress would insist on this implacable logic being applied. While they continued to talk publicly of a six-province Pakistan, privately they were resigned, by 1946, to getting, at best, something much less – what Jinnah referred to derisively as 'a shadow and a husk, a maimed, mutilated and moth-eaten Pakistan' [60 *pp. 415–16*]. If the choice came down to ruling a small, feeble state or sharing power with Congress in a great all-India state, Jinnah for one favoured the latter.

Accordingly, the Council of the Muslim League in June 1946 voted to accept the Cabinet Mission Scheme, implicitly repudiating the sovereign Pakistan option. However, this last chance reprieve for the principle of a united India was destroyed by the thoughtless intervention of a single individual: Jawaharlal Nehru. On 11 June, shortly after taking up the reins of the Congress presidency for a fourth time, Nehru held a press conference at which he offered the casual observation that the grouping provision should be considered a transitional arrangement pending the drafting of a popular constitution. The remark confirmed the League's deep-seated suspicion that Congress's democratic rhetoric masked a totalitarian lust for centralised power [*Doc. 32*]. At once the party cancelled its acceptance of the Cabinet Mission Scheme and reiterated its demand for Pakistan – a demand which Jinnah indicated would now be pursued in the streets as well as in the legislatures. 'Never have we, in the whole history of the League, done anything except by constitutional methods…', an emotional Quaid-i-Azam thundered. 'But now … we bid goodbye to constitutional methods' [68 *p. 344*]. A few weeks later Jinnah made good his threat when he called upon all Muslims to observe 16 August 1946 as 'Direct Action Day'. Particularly in Bengal, where the day was recklessly gazetted as a public service holiday by League premier H.S. Suhrawardy, communal violence erupted almost immediately. Elsewhere the violence was contained by the police, but in Calcutta the city's largely Muslim constabulary, presumably acting on orders, turned a blind eye to the mayhem. Three days later 6,000 Calcutta citizens were dead and at least 20,000 seriously injured – most of them, ironically, Muslims.

Having unleashed a Juggernaut, Jinnah contritely pleaded with his followers to exercise restraint. But his voice now carried no more authority with the mob than did those of his Congress counterparts – Nehru, Patel and Maulana Azad. In September 1946 the bloodlust spread to Bombay, thence in October to Dacca, the east Bengal district of Noakhali and rural Bihar, and early in the new year to Ahmedabad in Gujarat and Lahore and Rawalpindi in the Punjab. By 1947 north India was in the grip of an undeclared civil war between Muslims and non-Muslims, a war which, over the next eight months, would claim the lives of at least another 900,000 people and turn some twelve millions more into homeless refugees.

It is tempting to say that there were no winners from this holocaust, only losers; but that would not be quite true. Indirectly, the violence advanced the purposes of the League. When the King's cousin, Lord Louis Mountbatten, took up the viceregal reins in March 1947 in succession to Wavell, his official brief was to transfer power on the basis of the Cabinet Mission Scheme, or something close to it. However, a few tense meetings with a stoney-faced Jinnah persuaded him that the League would be satisfied with nothing short of a full division of the country. This left Mountbatten with the seemingly impossible task of persuading the INC to agree to something they had always, in the past, steadfastly resisted, and, true to form, Gandhi met his arguments with the grimly prophetic remark that if the partition went ahead it would probably have to take place over his dead body.

However, the Mahatma's views now carried much less weight in the councils of the Congress than those of his one-time deputies Nehru and Patel, and the latter responded more pragmatically. Shocked by the spreading violence and mindful (as was the viceroy) of the deteriorating efficiency of the security forces, they indicated to him as early as April that they might not oppose the establishment of Pakistan so long as the Hindu and Sikh minorities in Bengal and the Punjab were given the right to opt out, and on condition that the viceroy used his influence with the princes to persuade them to integrate their states in the Indian dominion. (If all or most of the states acceded, India would pick up more territory than it stood to lose to Pakistan.) Patel defended the foreshadowed partition publicly as a form of drastic surgery to 'remove the diseased limb'. (Privately he let it be known that he expected Pakistan to disintegrate within a matter of months.) On 3 June the party leaders went on All-India radio to announce that they had reached agreement with the viceroy for a transfer of power on these terms.

It was not quite a *fait accompli*. Congress insisted that the 3 June agreement be subject to ratification by 'the Indian people'. Yet the pro-cedure employed to solicit the public's opinion made a mockery of this commitment. The crucial decision as to whether the Punjab and Bengal should be partitioned was placed in the hands of the Muslim and Hindu members of the two provincial legislatures, sitting separately. Given the limited nature of the electorate under the 1935 Act – barely 10 per cent of the population – this hardly amounted to a democratic choice. Moreover, the 'yes' case needed the assent only of a simple majority of either group to be carried, and Congress had already instructed its MLAs to vote as a block for partition. But that, perhaps, was not the worst of it. While the parliamentary route was deemed good enough for Punjab and Bengal, when it came to deciding the fate of the NWFP, the government reverted to the mechanism of a direct plebiscite of voters. The reason? The NWFP legislature had a Congress majority. A simple poll of legislators might have achieved the wrong result. As it was, only 50.99 per cent of the province's registered electors cast their votes in favour of joining Pakistan.

In his statement to parliament on 20 February, Attlee announced that Britain planned to withdraw from India in June 1948. In June Mountbatten was authorised to bring the handover forward by some ten months to 15 August 1947, a tacit acknowledgement that the once all-powerful Raj was fast disintegrating. This left very little time for the government to decide how the country's administrative assets should be divided up, to physically move Pakistan's share to its interim capital Karachi, and to demarcate the boundary between the two dominions. Many Indian historians believe that this policy of 'scuttle' contributed significantly to the chaos that attended the partition of the Punjab, while many Pakistani historians have questioned whether due process was followed by Sir Cyril Radcliffe's boundary commission, which for reasons never explained allotted part of the Muslim-majority district of Gurdaspur to India, thereby giving it land access to Kashmir. Contemporaries, however, were more generous. Mountbatten's last official progress through New Delhi as viceroy on the morning of 15 August was repeatedly halted by the crush of jubilent crowds, while British onlookers that day, some of them sun-dried veterans of brutal encounters with the nationalists, found themselves hugged and garlanded by smiling strangers. 'We have never been so popular', one of them remarked wryly.

MOTTLED DAWN

At the beginning of this book I spoke about turning points and how these have been used by historians to shape their narratives. The handover of power on 15 August 1947 was clearly a major turning point in some respects, and has been recognised as such in dozens of standard works. Yet just as continuities overshadowed changes in the Indian scene of 1885, so the India of the 1950s and 1960s continued to be influenced by the patterns and structures laid down during the late colonial period. For one thing, not all the British immediately went home. Mountbatten himself stayed on for a year at Nehru's behest as a constitutional governor-general, while the governors of the Punjab, Madras, Bombay and the NWFP, several service chiefs, and eighty-three civilian officers remained in their jobs until at least the end of the decade. As late as the 1970s the tea industry was still largely in British hands. Imperial influence survived, too, in the British-trained Indian members of the Indian Administrative Service (IAS) which succeeded to the governing responsibilities of the ICS in 1947. Twenty years on, nineteen out of twenty-three heads of the Indian central secretariat department were headed by former ICS-*wallahs*. The last British-trained IAS officer only retired in 1980. Thirdly, for several years both countries continued to be governed in accordance with the legal norms of the Act of 1935, and many of these were directly imported into the Indian Constitution which passed into law in 1950. Indeed, the two documents have about 250 identical clauses. Last but not least, continuity was preserved in a vast web of inherited administrative forms and guides: training manuals; codes of criminal and civil procedure; the designations of 'district officer', 'chief commissioner', 'high court'; revenue records; railway timetables; maps and gazetteers; law reports. All of these, what is more, were written principally in English – the only language which, to this day, has elite currency throughout the subcontinent.

But it is not only the political forms that have persisted; the successor regimes have also aped the Raj's authoritarian style. In Pakistan and to some extent also in Bangladesh after 1971, this took the form of an imposition of martial rule for extended periods. While India has not so far gone down this track, it came close during Indira Gandhi's Emergency of 1975–77. More insidiously, perhaps, Indian federal governments have regularly made use of the provision in the Constitution (one of those borrowed directly from the 1935 document) that allows the president in certain circumstances to dismiss elected state governments and impose direct rule from the centre. Similarly, perceived threats to the integrity of the state have always been met with exemplary force. One of Sardar Patel's first acts as Home Minister was to ban the CPI, which was inciting the peasants of Andhra to overthrow their landlords. When war with China broke out in 1962, Nehru's Congress government introduced a Defence of India Act identical in name and very similar in content to one he himself had denounced as a young man. In the early 1980s Indira Gandhi sent in troops to root out Sikh separatists holed up in the Golden Temple in Amritsar. And in the 1990s up to half a million troops were deployed against Muslim militants in Kashmir.

Moreover, thanks to Mountbatten's accelerated timetable for the transfer of power, the British in 1947 left behind them numerous unresolved (and in some cases potentially insoluble) problems, of which the most immediate was the refugee problem. Displaced by the whim of Radcliffe's pen, millions of terrified Hindus, Muslims and Sikhs thronged the railway stations and the bus depots in late August 1947, desperately looking for a passage to safety. Those who could not afford tickets simply shouldered what meagre possessions they could carry and walked. Perhaps three-quarters of a million were butchered en route; and of those who survived, several hundred thousand women and girls were raped or abducted, many never to be reunited with their families [*Doc. 33*]. Based in a Calcutta slum, Gandhi fought against the tide in the only way he knew how, threatening to fast to death unless communal leaders agreed to halt the killing; but while his presence helped to keep the peace in Calcutta, other cities like Delhi erupted. In August 1947 and for several months afterwards, the Mahatma teetered on the edge of despair.

Partition sowed other deadly seeds too. The Hindu Mahasabha, condemning the settlement of 1947 as a national betrayal, demanded that the Congress Union government stop transferring assets to Pakistan. But while he deeply regretted the injury that had been done to his beloved homeland, Gandhi was adamant that the debt to Pakistan had to be paid, and in March 1948 he announced that he planned to embark on another indefinite fast to ensure that the Indian government fulfilled its legal and moral obligations. The Mahasabha and the RSS denounced this plan as tantamount to treason. In the early evening of 30 March, as he addressed a prayer meeting at Birla House, New Delhi, India's prince of peace was shot and killed by a member of an RSS splinter-group, Nathuram Godse.

However, if the Hindu Right felt cheated by the settlement of 1947, the same could be said for many Muslims. For supporters of the Muslim League, the triumph of Pakistan was marred by the restricted compass of the new state, which excluded many of their co-religionists. While some of the latter were able to make their way to Pakistan as refugees, more than 30 millions chose, or were forced by economic circumstance, to remain in India, their presence a glaring indictment of the two-nation theory. Bengali Muslims, too, had mixed feelings about Pakistan. Many would have preferred to join a separate Bengali state defined by culture rather than religion. These reservations intensified when the Pakistan government announced that Urdu would be the country's sole official language. By 1952 Bengalis were rioting in the streets against Punjabi linguistic 'imperialism'. As for those Muslims who did get to Pakistan, the *muhajirs* as they are called, the promised land proved, in many cases, less than welcoming. By their nature, the *muhajirs* tended to be better educated and more wealthy than the local Sindhis and Punjabis, and they quickly filled most of the important posts in the new government. The locals vented their rage by attacking *muhajir* persons and property. One of the early victims of this vendetta was the country's first prime minister, Liaquat Ali Khan, assassinated in 1951.

Perhaps the major losers in 1947, though, were the Sikhs. As a tightly-knit and well-organised religious group, residing mainly in the Punjab, the

Sikhs believed, with some justification, that they, too, were entitled to a separate homeland. During the war the main Sikh political party, the Akali Dal, formally lodged a claim to this effect [*Doc. 34*]. But for all its moral force, the Dal's homeland claim was fatally flawed by geography. The only possible location for the putative Sikh state, Khalistan, was the central Punjab, a region already claimed by the Muslims for Pakistan. Moreover, the Sikhs living within this region were widely and thinly dispersed; nowhere did they amount to a majority of the population. Accordingly, their claim for statehood was rejected. But the Akali Dal refused to give up its dream, and as the date for the British withdrawal drew near, it clandestinely assembled caches of arms with a view to establishing Khalistan by force. One aspect of this scheme was the ethnic cleansing of the central and eastern Punjab of Muslims, a project whose terrible consequences have already been noted. Nevertheless, for all its calculated brutality, the coup failed, leaving the Sikhs with no alternative but to seek refuge in the security of Indian-controlled east Punjab.

1947, then, was a year of transition rather than one of abrupt discontinuity and closure. But in the way of transitions, every year that has passed since 1947 has seen an imperceptible but steady weakening of the British legacy. One of the first things to go was the residual authority of the Crown. As we have seen, the various parties agreed, for pragmatic reasons, that power should be transferred on the basis of dominion status. However, the British government indicated that it would raise no objections if either dominion chose at a later date to sever its remaining ties with the Crown, and both states lost no time in availing themselves of this invitation. In 1950 India formally transformed itself into a republic. Racked by division, Pakistan moved more slowly, but in 1956 it, too, became a republic.

The colonial economic nexus also dissolved quickly, as the case of India shows. As late as the 1970s the bilateral trade pattern between Britain and India still had a colonial stamp: agricultural commodities inwards, manufactures outwards. But the scale of this trade fell sharply during the 1960s. By 1970 it was worth less than half what it had been twenty years earlier. Moreover, the two countries now traded more extensively with other parts of the world than they did with each other. By the 1980s less than 6 per cent of India's imports came from the United Kingdom, and just 9 per cent of its exports went there.

However, the most important break with the past after 1947 took place in the area of public policy. The British left behind a subcontinent undeveloped and partially modernised. In 1951 male literacy was 24 per cent, female literacy just 8 per cent. Life expectancy was a mere thirty-four years. As late as 1961 there were only ten doctors for every 100,000 people. Their constitutional reforms had laid the foundations for a representative democracy, but had fallen far short of enfranchising the mass of the population.

In the eighteenth century India had led the world in the production of textiles; in 1951 less than 3 per cent of India's labour force was employed in mines or factories, compared to 75 per cent in agriculture. The stark inequalities of the Hindu caste system were as deeply entrenched at the end of British rule as they were at its beginning. These deficiencies reflected the way the British had ruled: in the way of an umpire or manager rather than as a conscious agent of development. The successor governments had a different vision and a greater sense of social responsibility. Quickly India moved to the implementation of full democracy; the 1950 Constitution conferred the right to vote on all adults, literate and non-literate alike. At the first general election of 1951–52 over 100 million people exercised their franchise, easily a world record. The Constitution also committed Indian governments to introduce programmes to ameliorate social disadvantage, and untouchables were marked out for special attention in a schedule to the main document. Meanwhile, land reform legislation was introduced in several states in an attempt to break up the estates of the big *zamindars*; and a Soviet-style Planning Commission was established to ensure that scarce funds were channelled into areas of greatest need, such as primary education and heavy industry. To be sure, outcomes did not always match expectations – particularly in respect of land reform. Nevertheless, India's progress since 1947 has been remarkable. By 1991 literacy was 54 per cent nationally. Today India is once again an economic giant (ranked fourth in the world by size), producing, among other things, sophisticated computer software. By comparison, Pakistan's record has been more uneven, especially on the political front. Yet it, too, has been transformed. Little more than half a century has passed since the transfer of power, yet India and Pakistan are already virtually unrecognisable from the countries that emerged in 1947 from the chrysalis of British colonialism.

However, change has not entirely erased the imprint of South Asia's colonial past. For one thing, a few concrete legacies still remain: the descendants of Anglo-Indian marriages, lost between cultures; cricket; the English language, now studded with Hindustani words; the international imbroglio over Kashmir, which was one of the very few princely states to elude Mountbatten's grasp in 1947. More importantly, the period lives on in countless British, Indian and Pakistani memories: memories nourished by the heroic tales handed down within families, by books and films, and, in the subcontinent, by strongly nationalistic history-teaching in schools. These memories might not be very reliable, but they are vivid and they stir passions: as Queen Elizabeth found when she visited Amritsar in 1997 in the course of a tour to celebrate the fiftieth anniversary of Indian independence, and was met by a demand that she offer an official apology for the Jallianwallah Bagh massacre of 1919.

CHAPTER SIX

THE GIFT OF FREEDOM

In 1885 the Indian subcontinent was a valued dependancy of the British Crown and looked likely to remain such for an indefinite period, certainly for a longer time than any Indians or Britons of that era could imagine. Seventy years later the subcontinent was free and the Indian Empire a fading memory. Explaining this turnaround constitutes the central problematic of modern Indian (and Pakistani) history.

For a long time interpretations of the transfer of power clustered around two polar but equally Whiggish views, which can be labelled neo-imperialist and nationalist. In the neo-imperialist conception, India and Pakistan gained their freedom as the result of an act of British benevolence, undertaken to redeem a long-standing imperial commitment. As one typical exposition, by former ICS officer Sir Percival Griffiths, has it, 'Other ruling powers have abdicated after defeat in war or as a result of successful insurrection, but it was left for Britain to surrender her authority of set purpose and as part of a process of [d]evolution which had been operating for some decades' [44 *p. 356*]. The nationalist view, on the other hand, holds that power was not so much devolved, as seized. The British left, runs this interpretation, because by the 1940s they no longer possessed the means or the will to resist the implacable tide of the popular movement unleashed against them by the Congress and its allies.

Neither explanation, however, cuts much ice today. Hard pressed though they may have been, the British never completely lost control over the subcontinent. Conversely, for all that they put the Raj under great strain, it cannot be said that the nationalists ever managed physically to break Britain's imperial grasp. Power was not seized, at least in the sense that we can say that it was seized from the French in Indochina or, with a little more qualification, from the Dutch in the East Indies. There was no defining revolution. To this extent, Griffiths is right in talking about abdication. In 1947 the Congress and the Muslim League acceded to power in Delhi and Karachi by virtue of an act of the imperial parliament at Westminster. What is more, the major party leaders all agreed that it should happen that way, even though the process entailed some degree of political compromise on their part. While it might be stretching the point to suggest, as numerous Leftist writers have done, that the Congress and Muslim League high commands went along with London's proposal for an early transfer of power on the basis of dominion status as a way of forestalling a genuine social revolution, there is no denying that the conservative nature of the 1947 settlement benefited the Indian bourgeoisie.

That said, however, Griffiths' claim that the British devolved power of their own volition simply does not bear examination. For one thing the notion is implausible. States by their nature do not give up their power willingly. For another, it does not sit with the evidence now available as a result of the opening to scholars of the relevant government archives. Down to 1914 there is not the slightest hint in the archival record that the British were liberalising the constitution as a way of moving the country by stages towards self-government. (As late as 1912, it will be remembered, Hardinge was talking boldly about the permanence of British rule in the subcontinent.) And I think the same can be said, though more tentatively, of the reform process between 1917 and 1935. The pledge of 1917 was vitiated by the deliberate omission of any target-date for transferring power. Indeed, Curzon's gloss on the expression 'ultimate self-government', as employed by the Cabinet in 1917, was that it presumed 'an intervening period of 500 years' [74 *p. 31*]. Not until 1942 did Britain commit even to a notional time-frame, and then its offer was conditional, a 'post-dated cheque', as K.M. Panikkar waspishly remarked, 'drawn on a failing bank' [51 *p. 298*]. Conversely, a lot of archival evidence *has* been found for the proposition that the substantive reforms introduced by the British in 1919 and 1935 were carefully crafted to buttress the Raj by broadening its appeal to the public.

Of course modern interpretations encompass and accommodate elements of these older discourses – and necessarily so. After all, it would be hard to imagine a history of decolonisation in South Asia that did not speak of the freedom struggle or consider the impact of British constitutional reforms. But the modern accounts are much more critical in the way they interpret the actions of the British, the Congress and the League. Today's scholars are inclined to be more sceptical of surface explanations; they look for ulterior motivations that were deliberately kept hidden at the time. And thirty years of archival access has provided them with plenty of ammunition. Nevertheless, as one might expect, scholarly opinion remains bitterly divided about exactly why decolonisation happened at the time and in the manner that it did.

During the 1970s and 1980s many historians, particularly from British universities, ran with the theme of imperial self-interest, arguing that by the 1940s the British could rationally contemplate 'giving away' the Indian

Empire: first, because South Asia was no longer as crucial as it had once been to the maintenance of the United Kingdom's economic prosperity; and secondly because they no longer saw formal political control as an essential prerequisite for doing profitable business there. A varient on this theory postulated that, in a climate of shrinking resources, post-war Britain took a conscious decision to extricate itself from responsibilities in India, the more successfully to focus on regions that were now more vital to its global power and prestige, such as the oil-rich Middle East. Other scholars, meanwhile, drawing instructive lessons from a close study of those institutions that made up the 'steel frame' of British control in India, the ICS and the Indian Army, pointed to the importance of the bureaucratic factor in the decision to decolonise. By the 1940s, the argument ran, both the civilian and (to a lesser extent) the military services had become seriously degraded, leaving the Raj so exposed that the British government had no option but to wind it up. Finally, a group of Cambridge-based historians, of whom Anil Seal, Anthony Low and the late John Gallagher are perhaps the best known, taking as their intellectual starting point the premise of collaboration, contended that the British were forced out of the game by the defection or enfeeblement of key support-groups (such as the Muslims and the land-lords) and more generally by a withdrawal of popular consent, made dramatically manifest in the elections of 1936 [50, 75].

Since then, however, there has been something of a reaction against the cynical assumptions ingrained in this writing. In a partial return to the neo-imperialist view that Britain's withdrawal from India honoured a long-held national commitment to democratic values, Brasted and Bridge, among others, have pointed to the notable contribution in this regard made by the British Labour Party. Labour's decision to transfer power, they show, was no tawdry concession to *realpolitik*, but the consequence of a genuine commitment that had been restated many times. According to this interpretation, India might well have gained its freedom even earlier had not the war intervened, delaying the installation of a majority Labour government until 1945 [73]. Similarly, narratives written from the Indian side, which, in contrast to the majority produced overseas, have always placed the contribution of the nationalist movement at centre stage, have in recent years placed renewed emphasis both on the part played by inspiring ideals (nationhood, liberty, equality of opportunity) in driving the freedom struggle, and on the very substantial impact of mass agitation by subaltern elements on the Raj's capacity to govern. This too is a very useful corrective, challenging as it does the notion implicit in much of the Cambridge School's work that agency lay primarily with the government rather than with its opponents.

But perhaps the most interesting recent work on the end of empire in South Asia has dealt with the Pakistan movement and the causes of partition. Of all the major Indian politicians, Mohammad Ali Jinnah has seemed by far the most inconsistent. How did a man who started political life in the Congress, who married a Parsi, who flouted many Islamic taboos and was at best irregular in his devotions, end up as the head of a Muslim and putatively Islamic state? What turned this moderate constitutionalist into an exponent of mass agitation? The orthodox Pakistani view is that Jinnah's transformation into the Quaid-i-Azam was a genuine one, forced upon him by the perfidy of Congress. It makes no allowance for guile or deception. But recent work, in particular by the Cambridge graduate Ayesha Jalal, squarely challenges this assumption. Jalal reviewed all the official and private papers pertaining to the Quaid-i-Azam's leadership of the League between 1937 and 1947. Not only did she find no convincing evidence of a transformation in Jinnah's beliefs, she found many hints that his adoption of the Pakistan cause was simply a bargaining tactic, designed to bluff the government and the Congress into conceding what he really wanted, which was a settlement that truly respected the constitutional rights of the Muslim minority. But the bluff was called, leaving Jinnah to contemplate what might have been had he played his hand better [48]. Needless to say, Jalal's conclusion that Pakistan was an accident born of misjudgement has not been well-received by historians from that part of the subcontinent. Nor has it gone down well with some Western scholars, who find the notion that Jinnah consistently said things he did not mean downright perverse. Yet Jalal's work resolves what is otherwise a jarring paradox. It gives Jinnah's life a unity it lacks in the hageographic accounts generated by his countrymen. It also helps us to make sense of what otherwise looks like a further change of mind, when, on the eve of independence, Jinnah told the Pakistan Constituent Assembly that he wanted Pakistan to be a place in which Muslims and Hindus could live harmoniously side by side, common citizens of a secular state [*Doc. 35*].

The 'industrial revolution' that has taken place during the last forty years in archival-based studies of South Asia has added layers of complexity to the story of the end of empire. No longer do monocausal theories of 'devolution' or 'freedom struggle' suffice on their own to explain how and why India and Pakistan gained their independence in 1947. Nevertheless, if the picture has become in some ways increasingly muddied and confused, certain core propositions are still valid, and may be reiterated by way of conclusion.

First, without the growth of a powerful and vocal Indian national movement there would have been no transfer of power. The exertions of the national movement in the end made it difficult, if not impossible, for the Raj to continue to administer the country effectively. Furthermore, and perhaps more importantly, the maturation of the Congress into a sophisticated and responsible political machine destroyed the major ideological pillar of British imperialism in South Asia, namely the claim that only foreigners could provide this large and diffuse region of the world with the just and benevolent rule it deserved. Secondly, the transfer of power happened when it did very largely because of external factors, notably the Second World War and the impact this had on Britain's capacity to continue to act as a front-rank imperial power. If the war had not intervened, it is likely that Britain would have adhered to its interwar timetable, which called for a departure sometime late in the century. Thirdly, power *was* handed over – not eagerly, perhaps, or as a gift without strings, but nonetheless in a way that reflected long-held British assumptions about the civilising purposes of empire. Macaulay in the 1830s had sought to provide retrospectively a justification for Britain's conquest of India; resuscitated in 1918 by Montagu and Chelmsford, his vision provided twenty years later a plausible justification for leaving.

Colonial rule by its nature can never be an absolute good. Nevertheless some colonialisms have been better than others. Britain's rule in India was less just than America's in the Philippines, but considerably more benevolent than that of its other modern rivals for the crown of empire, France and Holland, in Indochina and Indonesia. From that viewpoint, one of its chief redeeming features was the relatively gracious manner of its termination.

PART FOUR   DOCUMENTS

DOCUMENT 1   THE STANDARD OF LIVING, *c.* 1914

The standard of living among all classes of the population, especially among land-holders, traders and ryots, has increased very considerably in recent years, and extravagance on occasions of marriage and other social ceremonies has seriously increased. The average villager lives in a better house and eats better food than did his father; brass and other metal vessels have taken the place of coarse earthenware and the clothing of his family in quality and quantity has improved. We may also say that the increase in passenger miles travelled predicates the existence of spare money to pay for railway fares.

Official Report on the Enquiry into the Rise of Prices in India by K.L. Datta, in [1], pp. 135–6.

DOCUMENT 2   A VICEROY FLEXES HIS MILITARY MUSCLES, 1913

Everything seems to be going quietly in India at present except in Bengal where the dacoities are still very bad. I offered Carmichael [the governor of Bengal] two months ago the services of two regiments to help to put them down, but I have not yet had an answer from him to my proposal. In any case I intend to organise some big manoeuvres in the worst districts of Bengal during the winter, in which I shall collect all the British regiments and Artillery possible, in order that we may show them that we mean business, since the bulk of the population in that part of India has never seen a British 'Tommy'. We believe that the moral effect will be extremely good.

Lord Hardinge, Viceroy of India, to King George V, 26 July 1913, in [9], pp. 158–9.

DOCUMENT 3   THE MYTH OF THE 'HEAVEN BORN'

Our life in India, our very work more or less, rests on illusion. I had the illusion, wherever I was, that I was infallible and invulnerable in my dealing with Indians. How else could I have dealt with angry mobs, with cholera-stricken masses, and with processions of religious fanatics? It was not conceit, Heaven knows: it was not the prestige of the British Raj, but it was the illusion which is in the very air of India. They expressed something of the idea when they called us the 'Heaven born', and the idea is really make believe – mutual make believe. They, the millions, made us believe we had a divine mission. We made them believe they were right. Unconsciously perhaps, I may have had at the back of my mind that there was a British Battalion and a Battery of Artillery at the Cantonment near Ajmere; but I never thought of this, and I do not think that many of the primitive and simple Mers [tribe living in eastern Rajasthan] had ever heard of or seen English soldiers. But they saw the head of the Queen-Empress on the rupee, and worshipped it. They had a vague conception of the Raj, which they looked on as a power, omnipotent, all-pervading, benevolent for the most part but capricious, a deity of many shapes and many moods.

Sir Walter Lawrence, quoted in [71], p. 54.

DOCUMENT 4 LORD LYTTON PROPOSES AN ALLIANCE WITH THE INDIAN ARISTOCRACY

I am convinced that the fundamental political mistake of able and experienced Indian officials is a belief that we can hold India securely by what they call good government; that is to say, by improving the condition of the ryot, strictly administering justice, spending immense sums on irrigation works, &c. Politically speaking, the Indian peasantry is an inert mass. If it ever moves at all, it will move in obedience not to its British benefactors but to its native chiefs and princes, however tyrannical they may be. ... To secure completely, and efficiently utilise, the Indian aristocracy is, I am convinced, the most important problem now before us. I admit that it is not easy of immediate solution. For whilst, on the one hand, we require their cordial and willing allegiance, which is dependent on their sympathies and interests being in some way associated with the interests of the British power, on the other hand we certainly cannot afford to give them any increased political power independent of our own. Fortunately for us, however, they are easily affected by sentiment, and susceptible to the influence of symbols to which facts very inadequately correspond.

Lord Lytton, Viceroy of India to Lord Salisbury, 11 May 1876, in [22], pp. 20–1.

DOCUMENT 5 THOMAS STOKER ON HIS RELATIONS WITH THE PEASANTS

It is the object of every person who lives by the land to place the condition of himself and his industry before the Settlement Officer in the most disparaging light. It will be useless for me to say that the inquiry [into the resources of the district] has no connection with settlement; I will not be believed. I cannot divest myself of my official character. Every man whom I question will believe I am seeking a basis on which to assess his rent or revenue, and he will answer accordingly. He will declare that his fields do not return even the seed and labour, and that he and his family are starving. The evidence of my own sight will show him to be lying; but unless I make an inquisition and hunt up evidence, the record will misrepresent the facts.

And, indeed, the evidence being that of his fellows, will most likely support than contradict him. These are not mere speculations. I find ... that since I have been engaged in settlement work [fixing the land tax] my relations with the people are much changed. I am regarded as an enemy, to be opposed by their only weapon, that is to say, deception.

Thomas Stoker, Collector of Bulandshahr to the Commissioner of Meerut, quoted in [67], pp. 268–9.

DOCUMENT 6   LORD CURZON FORECASTS THE DEMISE OF THE CONGRESS

[Sir William] Wedderburn sent me a copy of the same document that he forwarded to you, and I answered him in very much the same spirit. He was anxious to extract from me some pronouncement that might be regarded as favourable to the Congress. Now I am not going to be tempted into anything of the sort. My own belief is that the Congress is tottering to its fall, and one of my greatest ambitions while in India is to assist it to a peaceful demise. I told him plainly, therefore, that I felt myself incapacitated from giving any opinion about, or offering any advice to, the Congress; but I added that, while I was myself sensible of the desirability of consulting and conciliating public opinion in India, the composition of the Congress, at any rate in recent years, had deprived them of any right to pose as the representative of more than a small section of the community. My belief is that the best men in the Congress are more and more seeing the hopelessness of their cause, and indeed many of their papers have begun to argue that they had better trust to me to give them as much as I can instead of wasting their energies in clamouring for what no Viceroy is likely to give them at all.

Lord Curzon, Viceroy of India, to Lord George Hamilton, 18 November 1900, in [19], pp. 150–1.

DOCUMENT 7   A BRITISH OFFICIAL ON THE VIRTUES OF THE MARTIAL RACES

In all parts of the Punjab the population is composed of distinct races living alongside of each other, but apart. Some have been ruling or fighting races in former days; others only men of the pen, traders, or artisans. At present these races differ greatly in average sharpness of intellect and in hereditary aptitude for acquiring book-learning of all kinds. And those who excel in these particulars are not, speaking generally, those who have the highest self-respect, or who are most distinguished for courage or manliness.

Suppose you went into any large school in the Punjab and made a selection of the most promising boys of each race, selecting such a number of boys of each race as would roughly agree with the numerical importance of the race in the population of the Division, the result as to numbers would be that the group of selected boys would contain more sons of the old ruling and fighting races, such as Hindu, Sikh, or Muhammadan Ràjputs, and Jâts, Pathàns, Moguls, Awàns, &c., than sons of the less warlike races, such as the hereditary traders, clerks, or artisans. But if you then submitted the whole group to a competitive educational examination, the chances are that all or almost all the top places would be taken by boys belonging to the minority. It seems very undesirable, especially in Revenue and Executive Departments that too many high officials should belong to a few, particular races, which races would in any crisis be found to form an insignificant item of the political forces of the country.

Note by J.B. Lyall, Financial Commissioner, Punjab, April 1883, in [4], Appendix: Evidence,
pp. 52–4.

DOCUMENT 8   TESTIMONY OF GENERAL DYER BEFORE THE DISORDERS INQUIRY COMMITTEE, 1919-20

Q. I think you had an opportunity to make up your mind while you were marching to decide what was the right course. You came to the conclusion that if there really was a meeting, the right thing for you would be to fire upon them straightaway?

A. I had made up my mind. I was only wondering whether I should do it or I should not.

Q. No question of having your forces attacked entered into your consideration at all?

A. No. The situation was very, very serious. I had made up my mind that I would do all men to death if they were going to continue the meeting. [...]

Q. Does it or does it not come to this; you thought that some striking act would be desirable to make people not only in Amritsar but elsewhere consider their position more correctly?

A. Yes. I had to do something very strong.

Q. You commenced firing the moment you had got your men in position?

A. Yes.

Q. The crowd had begun to go away when you continued firing?

A. Yes.

Q. The crowd were making an effort to go away by some of the entrances at the further end of the Bagh?

A. Yes.

Q. You put your pickets one to the right and one to the left of the entrance. Towards some places the crowd was getting thicker than other places?

A. They did.

Q. From time to time you changed your firing and directed it to places where the crowds were thickest?

A. That is so.

Q. Is that so?

A. Yes.

Q. And for the reasons you have explained to us you had made up your mind to open fire at the crowd for having assembled at all?

A. Quite right [...]

Q. I gather generally from what you put in your report that your idea in taking this action was really to strike terror? That is what you say. It was no longer a question of dispersing the crowd but one of producing a sufficient moral effect.

A. If they disobeyed my orders it showed that there was complete defiance of law, that there was something much more serious behind it than I imagined, that therefore these were rebels, and I must not treat them with gloves on. They had come to fight if they defied me, and I was going to give them a lesson.

Q. I take it that your idea in taking that action was to strike terror?

A. Call it what you like. I was going to punish them. My idea from the military point of view was to make a wide impression.

Q. To strike terror not only in the city of Amritsar, but throughout the Punjab?

A. Yes, throughout the Punjab. I wanted to reduce their *morale*; the morale of the rebels [...]

Q. What reason had you to suppose that if you had ordered the assembly to leave the Bagh they would not have done so without the necessity of your firing, continued firing for a length of time?

A. Yes I think it quite possible that I could have dispersed them, perhaps even without firing.

Q. Why did you not adopt that course?

A. I could disperse them for some time; then they would all come back and laugh at me, and I considered I would be making myself a fool.

Report of the Disorders Inquiry Committee, [3], Vol. 2, pp. 188–91.

DOCUMENT 9   MONTAGU AND CHELMSFORD EMBRACE THE
EDUCATED CLASS, 1918

We have seen it estimated that the number of people who really ask for free
institutions does not exceed 5 per cent of the population. It is in any case a
small proportion; but to the particular numeral we attach no importance
whatever. We are not setting about to stir 95 per cent of people out of their
peaceful conservatism and setting their feet upon a new and difficult path
merely at the bidding of the other 5 per cent; nor would that be our reason,
whether the articulate minority were 20 per cent or one-half per cent of the
whole. Our reason is the faith that is in us. We have shown how step by
step British policy in India has been steadily directed to a point at which the
question of a self-governing India was bound to arise; how impulses, at first
faint, have been encouraged by education and opportunity; how the growth
quickened nine years ago, and was immeasurably accelerated by the war.
We measure it not by the crowds at political meetings or the multiplication
of newspapers, but by the infallible signs that indicate the growth of
character. We believe profoundly that the time has now come when the
sheltered existence which we have given India cannot be prolonged without
damage to her national spirit; that we have a richer gift for her people than
any that we have yet bestowed on them; that nationhood within the Empire
represents something better than anything India has hitherto attained; that
the placid, pathetic contentment of the masses is not the soil on which such
Indian nationhood will grow, and that in deliberately disturbing it we are
working for her highest good.

Report on Indian Constitutional Reform [5], p.93.

DOCUMENT 10   THE SECRETARY OF STATE'S ANNOUNCEMENT OF
BRITISH POLICY, 20 AUGUST 1917

The policy of His Majesty's Government, with which the Government of
India are in complete accord, is that of the increasing association of Indians
in every branch of the administration and the gradual development of self-
governing institutions with a view to the progressive realisation of responsible government in India as an integral part of the British Empire. ... His
Majesty's Government have accordingly decided, with His Majesty's
approval, that I should accept the Viceroy's invitation to proceed to India to
discuss these matters with the Viceroy and the Government of India, to
consider with the Viceroy the views of local Governments, and to receive
with him the suggestions of representative bodies and others.

B.N. Pandey, [18], p. 105.

DOCUMENT 11 A 'DIEHARD' OFFICIAL DENOUNCES POLITICAL REFORM, 1930

In spite of the declarations of one British Government after another, in spite of accelerating the Simon Report, and in spite of all Your Excellency has done and said for them, hardly a handful of Indians, who should be the leaders of thought in India, have played the game or have shown themselves in any way fitted to lead the thoughts of the millions of illiterate people in the country – only a few Muhammadans have in any way responded to our advances, because they are in the minority.

Pray excuse me, Lord Irwin, for saying so bluntly what I think but it is not the time to say nothing or, worse still, what one does not believe, and none of us who know India can ever believe that you can graft a Western political system on to the oriental continent of India, unless some foreign power controls the man at the business end of the gun. And we further know that the so-called martial races will *not* serve under a Government of middle-class lawyer politicians and will await with confidence the appearance of a leader who will offer them the loot of India to put him on the throne at Delhi and believe me it would not long be delayed.

General Sir Philip Chetwode, Commander-in-Chief, India, to Lord Irwin, 6 May 1930, British Library: Oriental and India Office Collection, Manuscript EUR C152, Vol. 19.

DOCUMENT 12 ROMESH DUTT ON THE BURDEN OF TAXATION

The income of the people of India, per head, was estimated by Lord Cromer and Sir David Barbour in 1882 to be 27 rupees. Their present income is estimated by Lord Curzon at 30 rupees. Exception has been taken to both these estimates as being too high; but we shall accept them for our present calculation. 30 rupees are equivalent to 40 shillings; and the economic condition of the country can be judged from the fact that the average income of the people of all classes, including the richest, is 40 shillings a year against £42 a year in the United Kingdom. A tax of 4s. 8d. on 40 shillings is tax of 2s. 4d. on the pound. This is a crushing burden on a nation which earns very little more than its food. In the United Kingdom, with its heavy taxation of £144,000,000 (excluding the cost of the late war), the incidence of the tax per head of a population of 42 millions is less than £3 10s. The proportion of this tax on the earnings of each individual inhabitant (£42) is only 8d. in the pound. The Indian taxpayer, who earns little more than his food, is taxed 40 per cent more than the taxpayer of Great Britain and Ireland.

Romesh Dutt, [27], pp. 603–4.

DOCUMENT 13   THE 'ATROCITIES' OF THE PLAGUE OFFICERS IN POONA, *c.* 1896

Had they known that this [house to house] inspection [by the Bombay government's inspectors] meant only spoilation; that the white men carrying on that work were marauders with Colonel Phillips, Lewis and other white men as their ringleaders; that Mr. Rand was the chief in command over them; that it was merely for the sake of carrying on this premeditated and extensive loot that one Dr. Jones was appointed before hand; that as a preliminary step these English marauders had caused him to make large openings in the houses of the rich as well as of the poor with the only object of rendering visible, while on their raid in broad daylight, the treasury boxes and other articles placed in the dark; that like the Ramoshi dacoits of our own country, who first make careful inquiries [about the belongings of their victims] to enable them to commit dacoities during night, Dr. Jones had, at the outset, by means of a general inquiry, prepared a list of the rich as well as the poor people of the city and had handed it over to those marauders at the commencement [of the operations]; and that those marauders taking advantage of the mildness of the Hindus, were about to commence their pillage under the guise of law; in short, if the rayats [peasants] had known before hand that their paternal Government was about to cut the throats of their own subjects in the above manner, they would have, to save themselves, migrated to some other place with all their belongings. But as they failed to perceive this state of things before hand they remained in their homes [confident of their] security. Meanwhile a band of these marauders paid their first visit to Budhwar [Peth]. Immediately on their arrival, they stationed guards at the corner of the street and began to break open shops by picking the locks. Oh what a spectacle it was. Indeed, neither history nor tradition can show such treatment accorded to a subject people by their rulers. One can understand an army raised to meet an enemy being used in repelling an invading foe; but here we see our valiant Englishmen [utilising] their brave and well-equipped forces in swooping down upon moribund victims [of the plague] and packing them off to hospitals. How very brave of them. Would [any other] ruler on the face of the globe use his forces in such a fashion? Our English [rulers], however, appear to think that valour consists not in striking down a man in full possession of his powers, which any one can do, but in capturing those who are stricken with illness and are unable to move an inch. It is for this reason that they employed their well-drilled soldiers on such operations. In this way did these plunderers commence their depredations. We always followed the parties which carried on this plunder, with the object of seeing with our own eyes their high-handed proceedings. I prefer to call these operations a loot rather than inspection. While this loot was going on, high officers of Government with Mr. Rand at their head paraded in the streets and supervised the breaking of locks, the making away with furniture and other lawless proceedings and also saw that all these operations were duly carried on. They were at this time so much blinded with authority that they cared not for any Hindu gentleman, however high his position might be. Nothing but burning, demolition, wreckage and arrests were to be seen in those parts which this band of raiders visited. ...

Temples were desecrated in one part of the city, in another women were outraged and idols broken. The poor and the helpless were the greatest sufferers at the hands of these marauders.

From the 'Autobiography' of Damodar Chapekar, written in prison while awaiting execution, 1897, in [7], pp. 1007–9.

DOCUMENT 14 'UNITY IS STRENGTH'

...We would advise our countrymen in all parts of India to reflect that, if they ever aspire again to be a great nation and to restore their motherland to its former greatness, they must forget that they spring from various races and nationalities and learn now that they are children of the same soil. We must clearly see that it is only by insisting on the identity of our interests as the people of India ... that we can keep down and stamp out our provincial jealousies; and as to religious differences, they surely should not be allowed to stand in the way of the assertion of our political rights, since though differing in the forms of worshipping, we equally worship the same God. Whenever we shall be able to show one unbroken front of a united people of India, bound by a complete identity of interests and animated by a perfect similarity of aspirations, the hour of the regeneration of India to begin will surely have come. It should be the duty of all true patriots to inculcate in the popular mind by precept and example the imperative necessity of union and harmony to the welfare and progress of the native races.

Article in the *Liberal and New Dispensation* (Calcutta), 10 August 1884, in [53], p. 229.

DOCUMENT 15 A.O. HUME: WHY INDIA NEEDS THE CONGRESS

Do you not realise that by getting hold of the great lower middle classes before the development of the reckless demagogues, to which the next quarter of a century must otherwise give birth, and carefully inoculating them with a mild and harmless form of the political fever, we are adopting the only certain precautionary method against the otherwise inevitable ravages of a violent and epidemic burst of the disorder? I know that both in these provinces and the Punjab there are many officials – good men and true though not far-seeing – who are publicly and privately doing their utmost to impede the progress and hinder the happy development of this great and beneficent movement; but, Gentlemen, as they are good men, acting, though ignorantly, in all good faith, they will be very sorry later for this, and they will regret that before opposing they did not first take the trouble of thoroughly understanding the movement, ...

A.O. Hume, in [19], pp. 141–3.

DOCUMENT 16   ADDRESS GIVEN BY B.G. TILAK DURING THE SHIVAJI FESTIVAL, POONA, 1897

Let us even assume that Shivaji first planned and then executed the murder of Afzal Khan. Was this act of the Maharaja good or bad? This question which has to be considered should not be viewed from the standpoint of the Penal Code or even the Smritis [law books] of Manu or Yajnavalkya, or even the principles of morality laid down in the Western and Eastern ethical systems. The laws which bind society are for common men like yourselves and myself. No one seeks to trace the genealogy of a Rishi [legendary sage], nor to fasten guilt upon a king. Great men are above the common principles of morality. These principles fail in their scope to reach the pedestal of great men. Did Shivaji commit a sin in killing Afzal Khan? The answer to this question can be found in the *Mahabharata* itself. Shrimat Krishna's teaching in the *Bhagavad Gita* is to kill even our teachers and our kinsmen. No blame attaches to any person if he is doing deeds without being motivated by a desire to reap the fruit of his deeds. Shri Shivaji Maharaja did nothing with a view to fill the small void of his own stomach [from interested motives]. With benevolent intentions he murdered Afzal Khan for the good of others. If thieves enter our house and we have not sufficient strength in our wrists to drive them out, we should shut them up and burn them alive. God has not conferred upon the *Mlechhas* [a barbarian or foreigner] the grant inscribed on a copperplate of the kingdom of Hindustan. The Maharaja strove to drive them away from the land of his birth; he did not thereby commit the sin of coveting what belonged to others. Do not circumscribe your vision like a frog in a well. Get out of the Penal Code, enter into the extremely high atmosphere of the *Bhagavad Gita*, and then consider the actions of great men.

B.G. Tilak, in [15], p. 56.

DOCUMENT 17 GANDHI ON WESTERN CIVILISATION, 1907

It has been stated that, as men progress, they shall be able to travel in airships and reach any part of the world in a few hours. Men will not need the use of their hands and feet. They will press a button, and they will have their clothing by their side. They will press another button, and they will have their newspaper. A third, and a motor-car will be waiting for them. They will have a variety of delicately dished-up food. Everything will be done by machinery. Formerly, when people wanted to fight with one another, they measured between them their bodily strength; now it is possible to take away thousands of lives by one man working behind a gun from a hill. This is civilisation. Formerly, people worked in the open air only as much as they liked. Now, thousands of workmen meet together and for the sake of maintenance work in factories or mines. Their condition is worse than that of beasts. They are obliged to work, at the risk of their lives, at most dangerous occupations, for the sake of millionaires.

Formerly, men were made slaves under physical compulsion. Now they are enslaved by temptation of money and of the luxuries that money can buy. There are now diseases of which people never dreamt before, and an army of doctors is engaged in finding out their cures, and so hospitals have increased. This is a test of civilisation. Formerly, special messengers were required and much expense was incurred in order to send letters; today, anyone can abuse his fellow by means of a letter for one penny. True, at the same cost, one can send one's thanks also. Formerly, people had two or three meals consisting of home-made bread and vegetables; now, they require something to eat every two hours so that they have hardly leisure for anything else. ...

M.K. Gandhi, *Hind Swaraj* (*Free India*) in R. Iyer (ed.), *The Moral and Political Writings of Mahatma Gandhi*, Vol. 1: *Civilisation, Politics and Religion* (Oxford, 1986), pp. 213–14.

DOCUMENT 18 LORD CHELMSFORD ON GANDHI, 1919

Mr. Gandhi is a man of great saintliness of character, an ascetic, but hopelessly unpractical and unversed in everyday affairs. Your Majesty may remember that he was responsible for the Passive Resistance movement amongst the Indians in South Africa some ten years ago, and that it was with the very greatest difficulty that the South African Government of the time found themselves able to cope with him. Indeed, they were only able to do so by persuading him to leave South Africa. As a proof of the esteem in which Mr. Gandhi is held by even those who most strongly opposed his action, I may say that rumour has it that when he was imprisoned in South

Africa General Smuts used to visit him in prison to discuss philosophy with him. ... This is a digression, but it has this importance, that it shows the estimation in which Mr. Gandhi is held by everyone who comes across him, and this fact renders the task of dealing with him much more difficult than if he were a mere agitating politician.

Lord Chelmsford, Viceroy of India to King George V, 21 May 1919, in [9], p. 194.

DOCUMENT 19   GANDHI'S REASONS FOR LAUNCHING THE NON-COOPERATION MOVEMENT, 1920

It is not without a pang that I return the Kaiser-i-Hind gold medal, granted to me by your predecessor for my humanitarian work in South Africa, the Zulu War medal granted in South Africa for my war services as officer in charge of the Indian Volunteers Service Corps in 1906 and the Boer War medal for my services as Assistant Superintendent of the Indian Volunteer Stretcher-Bearer Corps during the Boer War of 1899. I venture to return these medals in pursuance of the scheme of non-cooperation, inaugurated today in connection with the khilafat movement. Valuable as these honours have been to me, I cannot wear them with an easy conscience so long as my Mussulman countrymen have to labour under a wrong done to their religious sentiments. Events, which have happened during the last month, have confirmed me in the opinion that the Imperial Government have acted in the khilafat matter in an unscrupulous, immoral and unjust manner and have been moving from wrong to wrong in order to defend their immorality. I can retain neither respect nor affection for such a Government. The attitude of the Imperial and Your Excellency's Governments on the Punjab question has given me an additional sense for grave dissatisfaction.

Your Excellency's light-hearted treatment of the official crime, your exoneration of [Lieutenant-Governor] Sir Michael O'Dwyer, Mr. Montagu's dispatch and above all the shameful ignorance of the Punjab events and the callous disregard of the feelings of the Indians betrayed by the House of Lords, have filled me with the gravest misgivings regarding the future of the Empire, have estranged me completely from the present Government and have disabled me from tendering as I have hitherto whole-heartedly tendered my loyal co-operation. In my humble opinion, the ordinary method of agitating by way of petitions, deputation and the like is no remedy for moving to repentance a Government so hopelessly indifferent to the welfare of its charge as the Government of India has proved to be.

In European countries, the condonation of such grievous wrongs as the khilafat and the Punjab would have resulted in a bloody revolution by the people. They would have resisted at all cost the national emasculation such as the said wrongs imply. But one half of India is too weak to offer a violent resistance and the other half is unwilling to do so. I have therefore ventured to suggest a remedy of non-cooperation, which enables those who wish to dissociate themselves from the Government and which, if it is unattended by violence and undertaken in an ordered manner, must compel it to retrace its steps and undo the wrongs committed.

Gandhi to the Viceroy of India, 1 August 1920, in [18], pp. 52–4.

DOCUMENT 20   THE SUSPENSION OF NON-COOPERATION, 1922

I must tell you that this was the last straw. My letter to the Viceroy was not sent without misgivings as its language must make it clear to anyone. I was much disturbed by the Madras doings, but I drowned the warning voice. I received letters both from Hindus and Mohammedans from Calcutta, Allahabad and the Punjab, all these before the Gorakhpur incident, telling me that the wrong was not all on the Government side, that our people were becoming aggressive, defiant and threatening, that they were getting out of hand and were not non-violent in demeanour. Whilst the Ferozepur Jirka incident is discreditable to the Government we are not altogether without blame. Hakimji complained about Bareilly. I have bitter complaints about Jajjar. In Shahajanpur too there has been a forcible attempt to take possession of the Town Hall. From Kanouj too the Congress Secretary himself telegraphed saying that the volunteer boys had become unruly and were picketing a High School and preventing youngsters under 16 from going to the school. 36,000 volunteers were enlisted in Gorakhpur, not 100 of whom conformed to the Congress pledge. In Calcutta Jamnalalji tells me there is utter disorganization, the volunteers wearing foreign cloth and certainly not pledged to non-violence. With all this news in my possession and much more from the South, the Chauri Chaura news ... came like a powerful match to ignite the gunpowder, and there was a blaze. I assure you that if the thing had not been suspended we would have been leading not a non-violent struggle but essentially a violent struggle. It is undoubtedly true that non-violence is spreading like the scent of the attar of roses throughout the length and breadth of the land, but the foetid smell of violence is still powerful, and it would be unwise to ignore or underrate it. The cause will prosper by this retreat. The movement had unconsciously drifted from the right path. We have come back to our moorings, and we can again go straight ahead. You are in as disadvantageous a position as I am advantageously placed for judging events in their due proportion.

Gandhi to Jawaharlal Nehru, 19 February 1922, in [18], pp. 55–6.

DOCUMENT 21   MANIFESTO OF THE 'YOUNG HOOLIGANS', 1928

We [the Congress Left] are prepared to subordinate our ideas to some extent, but there are one or two things on which we find it impossible to give up whatever the consequences may be. I have understood that in the programme of action as to what is to be done and what is not to be done there should be a compromise and we have to fit ourselves in with other people's reasoning and desire, but I have not heard of compromise about ideals, of giving up an ideal to suit another's fancy. I do submit, whether it be for two years or one year or for a day, giving up of the ideal is a serious thing, which represents that you are pulling down your flag and that is a very serious thing. You are welcome to do it if you want it but you must realise fully the national and international consequences of that and having realised that, if you are prepared to pull down the flag of independence then do so by all means; but then you must give us the liberty to hold on to that flag even though we may be in a minority in the country. This is a vital issue and we feel with regard to it that there can be no compromise. It is a matter with us of the deepest conviction, it is a matter with us of what we think is the honour of the country and I submit it should be a matter with this House and the Congress of the most vital consequence involving the honour of the country. ...

I am not aware of any such country which under similar circumstances had adopted deliberately and consciously the dominion ideal of government. I do not see why we should say we want the Dominion type of government – mind you, it is not offered to us, there is no mention of this on the other side: but by their acts and deeds you can see the insult offered to you when a Commission [the Statutory Commission] goes about your country adding insult to injury. Do you think that it is right to haul down the Swaraj flag and to go on talking of Dominion Status? Personally I think, from whatever point of view you look at it, either from the stand point of national honour or from the point of view of experience, if you accept Dominion Status it would be an extremely wrong and foolish act. ...

I submit to you honestly that if I have energy to serve the country, that energy oozes out of me at the very thought of Dominion Status. I cannot go about spending my energy and strength for Dominion Status. I do submit to you that there are many like me in this country who feel like that. You will find in all-India groups of organisations that are springing up full of energy and militant spirit and they promise to attain an early freedom for India. The question is, are you going to help the development of the militant spirit in the country? Are you going to help the development of this revolutionary spirit in the country or are you going to damp it and kill it in trying to bring about a compromise? Certainly it damps my spirit if you talk of Dominion Status and I can only judge others by my standard. The real thing in the world is not so much the question of struggle between India and England, the real conflict is between the two sets of ideals; and the question is, which set of ideals are you going to keep before the country? This is a conflict between imperialism and all that is not imperialism and if you look at it from that point of view, you cannot for one moment think of Dominion Status so long as Great Britain has the empire around her.

Jawaharlal Nehru's speech to the Subject's Committee of the Calcutta Congress, 27 December 1928, in S. Gopal (ed.), *Nehru: Selected Works*, Vol. 3 (Sangam Books, New Delhi, 1978), pp. 272–3.

DOCUMENT 22   SIR SAIYYID AHMAD KHAN ON THE DANGERS OF DEMOCRACY, 1887

Now, let us suppose the Viceroy's Council made in this manner. And let us suppose first of all that we have universal suffrage, as in America, and that everybody, chamars [untouchables] and all, have votes. And first suppose that all the Mahomedan electors vote for a Mahomedan member and all Hindu electors for a Hindu member, and now count how many votes the Mahomedan member has and how many the Hindu. It is certain the Hindu member will have four times as many because their population is four times as numerous. Therefore we can prove by mathematics that there will be four votes for the Hindu [against] every one vote for the Mahomedan. And now how can the Mahomedan guard his interests? It would be like a game of dice, in which one man had four dice and the other only one. In the second place, suppose that the electorate be limited. Some method of qualification must be made; for example, that people with a certain income shall be electors. Now, I ask you, O Mahomedans! Weep at your condition! Have you such wealth that you can compete with the Hindus? Most certainly not. Suppose, for example, that an income of Rs. 5,000 a year be fixed on, how many Mahomedans will there be? Which party will have the larger number of votes? I put aside the case that by a rare stroke of luck a blessing comes through the roof and some Mahomedan is elected. In the normal case no single Mahomedan will secure a seat in the Viceroy's Council. The whole Council will consist of Babu so-and-so Mitter, Babu so-and-so Ghose, and Babu so-and-so Chuckerbutty ... [laughter].

Speech at Lucknow, 28 December 1887, cited in [15], pp. 43–7.

DOCUMENT 23   THE GENESIS OF THE SIMLA DEPUTATION, 1906

I find that Mohammedan feeling is very much changed, and I am constantly getting letters using emphatic language, and saying that the Hindus have succeeded owing to their agitation, and the Mohammedans have suffered for their silence. The Mohammedans have generally begun to think of organizing a political association and forming themselves into political agitators. Although it is impossible for the Mohammedans, on account of their lack of ability and union and want of funds, to attain any success like the Hindus, and they are likely to lose rather than gain by such a course, it is yet impossible for anybody to stop them. The Mohammedans of Eastern Bengal have received a severe shock. I have got a letter from Syed Nawab Ali Chowdry of Dacca which gives utterance to the extremely sorrowful feeling prevailing there. He says: 'Up to now the Mohammedans of Bengal have been careless. They have now begun to feel the consequences of their carelessness. If only the Mohammedans of Bengal, instead of following the Government, had agitated like the Hindus and had enlisted the sympathies of the Mohammedans of the whole of India, and raised their voice up to the Parliament, they would never see these unfortunate consequences.'

This is only a brief quotation of what I am getting from the whole of India. These people generally say that the Policy of Sir Syed Ahmed Khan and that of mine has done no good to Mohammedans. They say that Government has proved by its actions that without agitation there is no hope for any community, and that if we can do nothing for them we must not hope to get any help for the [MAO] college, in short; the Mohammedans generally will desert us, because the policy of the college is detrimental to their interests. My dear Archbold, nobody can say that the present state of Mohammedan feeling is without its justification. The Liberal Government is at the bottom of it, and is responsible for it. I consider it a wrong policy arising out of the ignorance of the real conditions in India. Mr. John Morley is a philosopher and might well have been contented to give lessons in philosophy; and one cannot but feel sorry that the destiny of India has been placed in his hands.

Mohsin-ul-Mulk, Secretary, MAO College, Aligarh, to W.A.J. Archbold, College Principal,
[received] 24 August 1906, in [28], pp. 54–5.

DOCUMENT 24   **SOME CAUSES OF HINDU–MUSLIM COMMUNAL RIOTS: A BRITISH ASSESSMENT, 1893**

6. One of the causes to which this increasing incidence of riots is due is, in our opinion, beyond all doubt, the greater frequency of communication and the interchange of news by post and telegraph between different parts of the country. A riot which occurs in any place, even the most remote, is speedily heard of all over India. Exaggerated reports of what has happened are spread abroad, and as most newspapers belong to one or other of the contending parties, the accounts published are often highly coloured by partisanship. The natural effect is that in places where harmony has

generally prevailed between the two parties, controversies arise and hostility is engendered; and the example set in some distant town may thus be followed in a dozen other places where the people, but for the suggestion afforded by the example and the manner in which it is discussed, would have continued to live in mutual amity.

This rapid dissemination of news and increasing activity of controversy, carried on through the Press, by public meetings, and by the addresses of itinerant preachers, is in some respects a new feature in Indian life, and is one which is likely to grow and add considerably to the difficulties of administration.

7. Another cause which contributes to embitter the relations between the two great religions is the greater forwardness of the Hindus in the race of life and their more active participation in the spirit and practice of modern political organization. Education, as your Lordship is well aware, has made most progress among the Hindu portion of the community; while the Mahomedans have to a large extent, and until more recent times, stood aloof from instruction conveyed in English. Public employment and success in the legal and other professions have thus become, to a great degree, the exclusive possession of Hindus. For the same reasons the conduct of the newspaper press has fallen mainly into the hands of Hindus; and political agitation, as carried on in India, has therefore a generally Hindu complexion which, in a community where religion lies at the basis of all relations of life, is liable easily to degenerate into a cause of religious discord. The effect of the exclusion from public and private employment, from which the Mahomedans have suffered, has naturally been to embitter their minds against the Hindus, and reflections on their past state of supremacy contribute to keep this feeling alive.

8. A third cause which has contributed greatly to increase the frequency of dissensions is what has often been called the 'Hindu revival'. ... [The Hindu revival] – the essence of which is the drawing tighter of the bonds of Hindu discipline, and the inculcation of respect for Brahmans and of veneration for the cow – is a symptom of this reaction against the influx of Western ideas and habits, though it may also to some extent be possibly regarded as a protest against the freer slaughter of kine by Mahomedans to which we have adverted above. Its most marked features at the present moment are the active propagandism carried on by itinerant religious preachers, and the development of the societies for the protection of kine which now exist in most provinces of India, but especially in the eastern portions of the North-Western Provinces and Oudh, in the contiguous province of Behar, and in the Central Provinces. ...

Home (Public) Dispatch from the Governor-General in Council to the Secretary of State for India, 21 December 1893, National Archives of India, Foreign Department, Internal A, December 1894: nos 113–55.

DOCUMENT 25   M.A. JINNAH'S 14–POINT RESOLUTION OF 1929

The League, after anxious and careful consideration, most earnestly and emphatically lays down that no scheme for the future constitution of the government of India will be acceptable to Mussalmans of India until and unless the following basic principles are given effect to and provisions are embodied therein to safeguard their rights and interests:–

(1)   The form of the future constitution should be federal, with the residuary powers vested in the provinces.

(2)   A uniform measure of autonomy shall be granted to all provinces.

(3)   All legislatures in the country and other elected bodies shall be constituted on the definite principle of adequate and effective representation of minorities in every Province without reducing the majority in any Province to a minority or even equality.

(4)   In the Central Legislature, Mussalman representation shall not be less than one-third.

(5)   Representation of communal groups shall continue to be by means of separate electorates as at present, provided it shall be open to any community, at any time, to abandon its separate electorate in favour of joint electorate.

(6)   Any territorial redistribution that might any time be necessary shall not in any way affect the Moslem majority in the Punjab, Bengal and NWF Provinces.

(7)   Full religious liberty i.e., liberty of belief, worship and observance, propaganda, association and education, shall be guaranteed to all communities.

(8)   No bill or resolution or any part thereof shall be passed in any legislature or any other elected body if three-fourths of the members of any community in that particular body oppose such a bill, resolution or part thereof on the ground that it would be injurious to the interests of that community or in the alternative, such other method is devised as may be found feasible and practicable to deal with such cases.

(9)   Sind should be separated from the Bombay Presidency.

(10)   Reforms should be introduced in the NWF Province and Baluchistan on the same footing as in other provinces.

(11)   Provision should be made in the constitution giving Moslems an adequate share along with the other Indians, in all the services of the State and in local self-governing bodies having due regard to the requirements of efficiency.

(12)   The Constitution should embody adequate safeguards for the protection of Moslem culture and for the protection and promotion of Moslem education, language, religion, personal laws and Moslem charitable

institutions and for their due share in the grants-in-aid given by the State and by local self-governing bodies.

(13)   No cabinet, either Central or Provincial, should be formed without there being a proportion of at least one-third Moslem Ministers.

(14)   No change shall be made in the constitution by the Central Legislature except with the concurrence of the States constituting the Indian Federation.

M.A. Jinnah, [19], pp. 235–6.

DOCUMENT 26   'PAKISTAN RESOLUTION' MOVED AT THE LAHORE SESSION OF THE ALL-INDIA MUSLIM LEAGUE, 1940

RESOLUTION No. 1

... Resolved that it is the considered view of this Session of the All-India Muslim League that no constitutional plan would be workable in this country or acceptable to the Muslims unless it is designed on the following basic principles, viz, that geographically contiguous units are demarcated into regions which should be so constituted, with such territorial readjustments as may be necessary, that the areas in which the Muslims are numerically in a majority as in the North-Western and Eastern zones of India should be grouped to constitute 'Independent States' in which the constituent units shall be autonomous and sovereign.

That adequate, effective and mandatory safeguards should be specifically provided in the Constitution for Minorities in these units and in the regions for the protection of their religious, cultural, economic, political, administrative and other rights and interests, in consultation with them, and in other parts of India where the Mussulmans are in a minority adequate, effective and mandatory safeguards shall be specifically provided in the Constitution for them and other Minorities for the protection of their religious, cultural, economic, political, administrative and other rights and interests in consultation with them.

In [11], p.443.

DOCUMENT 27   A DEMONSTRATOR RECALLS AN ENCOUNTER WITH THE POLICE

The Congress Party was very active in Delhi and in India as a whole, and, with increasing age and experience, I began to see things differently. Before this, I had thought primarily in terms of what affected me personally and, secondarily, of what affected my parents and the community. Now the problem was much greater; it became a question of India as a whole, with the untouchables in the center. Above all, I realized I was a child of India, and, as such, it was right for me to take part in this movement. There was also another side to it: the breaking of the barrier between castes. If I wore a [white] Gandhi cap, no one would ask who I was. So far, I had not worn the cap for that purpose, because I knew that something deeper than the words of Congress must happen to change our Karma. What I saw in the movement was the seed of change that sooner or later had to germinate.

I had been in Delhi a few weeks when we had news that the Indian Theatre was showing the play 'Bharat' ['India']. One evening after work, a few of us went to see this play. By this time, I was wearing the Gandhi cap when off duty. The play was causing a great sensation in India, and, though the theatre was packed, we managed to get in somehow. It was designed to show the misery of Indian life and the impact of British tyranny. It was a fine piece of propaganda. The play was only half way through, when the police threw a cordon round the theatre; then there was panic. No one knew what to do; people pushed in every direction to get out, but the more they pushed the greater became the chaos. Then someone shouted, 'We will all die for India, Mahatma Gandhi Kee Jay' ['Hail to Mahatma Gandhi'], and we waited to see what would happen next. The police arrested everyone wearing Gandhi caps and closed the theatre. It took a few hours to calm the crowd, and those arrested were taken to the police station across the road. Here the police treated us very roughly, and most of us were beaten. I received three heavy strokes across my back and was then set free, as were most of the others. This experience made us feel that we were martyrs in a good cause, and there was no longer shame in being beaten or jailed.

Rabindra K. Hazari, [29], pp. 126–8.

DOCUMENT 28   A NATIONALIST VIEW OF THE WAR SITUATION

A remarkable echo of these instructions has recently been heard in the statement of Nayananjan Das Gupta of the Jugantar Party. When he was interrogated, after his arrest, Das Gupta stated that he had evaded the arrest in the hope that when the Axis powers occupy a part of India and the Allied troops have retreated, the Indian nationalists who succeeded in remaining at large would set up a national government in the occupied areas before the invading army could consolidate its position and declare it free India. Whoever won the war would be compelled to come to terms with that National Government.

D.A. Brayden, CTO, Baliganj, Calcutta, to G. Ahmed, Deputy Director, IB, 22 April 1942, in [8], p. 2.

DOCUMENT 29 PRESIDENT ROOSEVELT PUTS HIS OAR IN, 1942

The feeling is held almost universally that the deadlock has been due to the British Government's unwillingness to concede the right of self-government to the Indians notwithstanding the willingness of the Indians to entrust to the competent British authorities technical military and naval defence control. It is impossible for American public opinion to understand why, if there is willingness on the part of the British Government to permit the component parts of India to secede after the war from the British Empire, it is unwilling to permit them to enjoy during the war what is tantamount to self-government.

I feel that I am compelled to place before you this issue very frankly, and I know you will understand my reasons for doing this. Should the current negotiations be allowed to collapse because of the issues as presented to the people of America and should India subsequently be invaded successfully by Japan with attendant serious defeats of a military or naval character for our side, it would be hard to over-estimate the prejudicial reaction on American public opinion.

President Roosevelt to Prime Minister Winston Churchill, 12 April 1942, in [14], pp. 759–60.

DOCUMENT 30 LORD WAVELL OFFERS A PRAGMATIC ARGUMENT FOR BRITISH WITHDRAWAL, 1944

Our prestige and prospects in Burma, Malaya, China and the Far East generally are entirely subject to what happens in India. If we can secure India as a friendly partner in the British Commonwealth our predominant influence in these countries will, I think, be assured; with a lost and hostile India, we are likely to be reduced in the East to the position of commercial bag-men. ... The following seem to me to be the essential factors of the problem:

(i) When we started, 20 or 30 years ago, on the political reform of India, we laid down a course from which we cannot now withdraw. It may have been a mistaken course, and it would probably have been better to have prescribed economic development first; but I am afraid it is too late to reverse the policy now. And the general policy, of giving India self-government at an early date, was confirmed not long ago in the Cripps' offer.

(ii) Nor do I think that in any case we can hold India down by force. Indians are a docile people, and a comparatively small amount of force ruthlessly used might be sufficient; but it seems to me clear that the British people will not consent to be associated with a policy of repression; nor will world opinion approve it, nor will British soldiers wish to stay here in large

numbers after the war to hold the country down. There must be acquies-
cence in the British connection if we are to continue to keep India within
the Commonwealth.

(iii) India will never, within any time that we can foresee, be an efficient
country, organised and governed on western lines. In her development to
self-government we have got to be prepared to accept a degree of ineffic-
iency comparable to that in China, Iraq, or Egypt. We must do our best to
maintain the standards of efficiency we have tried to inculcate, but we
cannot continue to resist reform because it will make the administration less
efficient.

(iv) The present Government of India cannot continue indefinitely, or
even for long. Though ultimate responsibility still rests with His Majesty's
Government, His Majesty's Government has no longer the power to take
effective action. We shall drift increasingly into situations – financial,
economic, or political – for which India herself will be responsible but for
which His Majesty's Government will get the discredit. We are already in
the position that Indian Members of Council have a controlling voice, and
are increasingly aware of their power. The British Civil Services, on which
the good government of the country has up till now depended, might
almost be described as moribund, senior members are tired and dis-
heartened, and it will be extremely difficult after the war to secure good
recruits. ...

We cannot move without taking serious risks; but the most serious risk
of all is that India after the war will become a running sore which will sap
the strength of the British Empire. I think it is still possible to keep India
within the Commonwealth, though I do not think it will be easy to do so. If
we fail to make any effort now we may hold India down uneasily for some
years, but in the end she will pass into chaos and probably into other
hands.

Lord Wavell, Viceroy of India, to Winston Churchill, 24 October 1944, in [30], pp. 94–9.

DOCUMENT 31   THE CRIPPS' OFFER, 1942

His Majesty's Government, having considered the anxieties expressed in
this country and in India as to the fulfilment of the promises made in regard
to the future of India, have decided to lay down in precise and clear terms
the steps which they propose shall be taken for the earliest possible realisation of self-government in India. The object is the creation of a new Indian
Union which shall constitute a Dominion, associated with the United
Kingdom and the other Dominions by a common allegiance to the Crown,
but equal to them in every respect, in no way subordinate in any aspect of
its domestic or external affairs.

His Majesty's Government therefore make the following declaration:–

(a)   Immediately upon the cessation of hostilities, steps shall be taken to set up in India, in the manner described hereafter, an elected body charged with the task of framing a new Constitution for India.
(b)   Provision shall be made, as set out below, for the participation of the Indian States in the constitution-making body.
(c)   His Majesty's Government undertake to accept and implement forthwith the Constitution so framed subject only to:–

>   (i) the right of any Province of British India that is not prepared to accept the new Constitution to retain its present constitutional position, provision being made for its subsequent accession if it so decides. ...

With such non-acceding Provinces, should they so desire, His Majesty's Government will be prepared to agree upon a new Constitution, giving them the same full status as the Indian Union, and arrived at by a procedure analogous to that here laid down.

British Parliamentary Papers, Cmd. 6350 (1942), pp. 4–5.

DOCUMENT 32   **THE LEAGUE'S ABOUT-FACE ON THE CABINET MISSION SCHEME, 1946**

As regards the proposal embodied in the statements of the 16th and 25th of May of the Cabinet Delegation and the Viceroy, the Muslim League alone of the two major parties has accepted it.

The Congress have not accepted it because their acceptance is conditional and subject to their own interpretation which is contrary to the authoritative statements of the Delegation and the Viceroy issued on the 16th and the 25th of May. The Congress have made it clear that they do not accept any of the terms or the fundamentals of the scheme but that they have agreed only to go into the Constituent Assembly and to nothing else; and that the Constituent Assembly is a sovereign body and can take such decisions as it may think proper in total disregard of the terms and the basis on which it was proposed to be set up. Subsequently this was made further clear and beyond any doubt in the speeches that were made at the meeting of the All-India Congress Committee in Bombay on the 6th of July by prominent members of the Congress and in the statement of Pundit Jawaharlal Nehru, the President of the Congress, to a press conference on 10th July in Bombay and then again even after the debate in the Parliament in a public speech by him at Delhi on the 22nd of July. ...

Once the Constituent Assembly were summoned and met there was no provision or power that could prevent any decision from being taken by the Congress, with its overwhelming majority, which would not be competent for the Assembly to take or which would be *ultra vires* of it, and however repugnant it might be to the letter or the spirit of the scheme. It would rest entirely with the majority to take such decisions as they may think proper or suit them and the Congress have already secured by sheer numbers an overwhelming Hindu-Caste majority whereby they will be in a position to use the Assembly in the manner in which they have already declared, i.e. that they will wreck the basic form of the grouping of the Provinces and extend the scope, powers and subjects of the Union Centre which is con-fined strictly to three specific subjects as laid down in paragraph 15 and provided for in paragraph 19 of the statement of 16th May.

The Cabinet Delegation and the Viceroy collectively and individually have stated on more than one occasion that the basic principles were laid down to enable the major parties to join the Constituent Assembly, and that the scheme cannot succeed unless it is worked in a spirit of co-operation. The attitude of the Congress clearly shows that these conditions precedent for the successful working of the constitution-making body do not exist. This fact, taken together with the policy of the British Government of sacrificing the interests of the Muslim nation and some other weaker sections of the peoples of India, particularly the Scheduled Castes, to appease the Congress and the way in which they have been going back on their oral and written solemn pledges and assurances given from time to time to the Muslims, leaves no doubt that in these circumstances the par-ticipation of the Muslims in the proposed constitution-making machinery is fraught with danger and the Council, therefore, hereby withdraws its acceptance of the Cabinet Mission's proposals which was communicated to the Secretary of State for India by the President of the Muslim League on the 6th of June 1946.

Resolution No. 1 of the Council of the Muslim League, 29 July 1946, in [11], pp. 619–20.

DOCUMENT 33   THE DESTRUCTION OF THAMALI VILLAGE, RAWALPINDI, 6–13 MARCH 1947

Our village and all the other neighbouring villages had a mixed population; it was only our village that had two-thirds Sikhs, one-third Hindus and only four or five Muslim houses. They did mostly *gharelu*, household work. There were no Muslim landowners in our villages, the Sikhs owned all the lands; the Sikhs and the Hindus ... the Muslims were so few, only five or six families and they used to go along with us. In fact, there was one Khan or somebody. When the riots took place, he sent warning messages to the Hindus and Sikhs to save themselves because they were being surrounded.

Yes, he helped us. Gujjar Khan tehsil was about 12 miles away. We sent someone there to ask for help, to say that we're surrounded. Someone was sent to Rawalpindi as well, ... There were many villages, some ten or so that were wiped out in these riots, ... On 13 March 1947 the rioters totally finished, spoiled, looted and burnt our villages. ...

As I told you, we were children, and were studying, we didn't know anything. But we used to hear from others, particularly our elders who read newspapers, that there would be Partition, that Hindustan and Pakistan would be made, but we used to think what difference would it make to us? Earlier we had *angrz* [English] rulers, now we would have Muslims. Nobody thought they would have to leave, certainly not the common people. ...

The killers were all from outside. Yes, the local Muslim families may have joined in the looting, but the killers were all from outside. After all, the locals are known to one another, there are some kinds of relationships, links ... no, they might have joined in the looting, but they were not killers. Whatever they found they looted and even burnt, but killing, no – you know it happens even here. What do the leaders do? They breed *goondas* [toughs] and when they need them, they get people from outside, they use these *goondas*, and then the locals join in. The same style.

On the night of the twelfth, we left at 4.00 a.m., in the early hours of the morning. Our own family, all the people, we collected them in the *gurudwara* and got some men to guard them. We gave them orders to kill all the young girls, and as for the *gurudwara*, to pour oil on it and set it on fire.

We decided [this] among ourselves. We felt totally helpless ... so many people had collected, we were totally surrounded. If you looked around, all you could see was a sea of people in all four directions ... wherever the eye could reach, there were men. After all, you get frightened. At that time, around 4.00 p.m. in the afternoon on the twelfth, some families went away, the Muslims called them and said, come we'll save you. The others then collected in the *gurudwara*. They collected together to comfort each other. But then we found that we were helpless ... we had no weapons, whatever little we had they had taken. ... Then they took a decision in the *gurudwara* about all the young girls and women; two or three persons were assigned the duty of finishing them off. Those in the *gurudwara* were asked to set it on fire with those inside. Some of them (after all, people are scared to die) ran away ... all those who were in the *gurudwara* were killed. Of those who came away, some got killed, some were wounded; we also came away.

I was 16 years old, my brother was 9. Our Father was with us, but he was killed on the way. In the morning, we reached another village. There were some 40 of us left, and of the 40, 12 got there. The others were all killed. Then close by, there was Kallar camp, we were taken there, and then from there to Gujjar Khan camp. ...

First, we killed all the young girls with our own hands; kerosene was poured over them inside the *gurudwara* and the place was set on fire. ... Women and children, where could they go? There was another village, Thoa Khalsa, there they pulled everyone out and said we will convert you to Islam, either you agree or ... but they had not started to kill them. Close by there was a well and the women jumped into it. I think some 150 women jumped into the well and took their lives.

We came away around four o'clock ... [but] there were survivors. Some were killed, some survived. The next day we reached Kallar, the military took us. They asked about our families. ... There were some women who got frightened, some whose husbands were killed, so they hid and got away. ... The harvest, the wheat was ripe, so they hid in the wheat fields. Then in the morning the military arrived and took their children out. There was killing and arson. About the Congress and the Muslim League we don't know. About that, only the older leaders can tell you. We can only tell you the reality we witnessed, that's all.

From an interview with Simret Singh conducted by Urvashi Butalia and Sudesh Vaid, *c.*1993,

in [12], pp. 146–9.

DOCUMENT 34   THE SIKHS DEMAND A HOMELAND, 1946

The draft declaration provides for the right of non-accession of Provinces. The Sikhs make it plain that they are opposed to any possible partition of India as envisaged in the draft declaration. As stated above, the Sikhs form a compact cultural nationality of about six millions. They further maintain that, judged by any definition or test, the Punjab is not only their homeland, but their holy land. They were the last rulers of the Punjab and before the advent of the British they enjoyed in the Punjab independent economic and political status which has gradually deteriorated under British rule.

They wish, however, to point out that, with the inauguration of provincial autonomy on the basis of the Communal Award, they have been reduced to a state of complete helplessness. If the existing provincial political set-up is continued, the transference of power to the people would perpetuate the coercion of the Sikhs under what in practice has come to be Muslim rule. That set-up is unjust to the Sikhs. Its working has meant Muslim communal rule in the Punjab which has almost exasperated the Sikhs to the point of revolutionary protest. The intervention of war conditions alone has been responsible for the Sikhs acquiescing temporarily in this communal tyranny. They cannot be expected to continue to submit to it as a permanent arrangement in any new scheme of Indian polity.

Akali demands: The statutory Muslim majority in the Legislature of the Province must go and the position of the Sikhs must be strengthened by increased representation therein so as to ensure to the Sikhs an effective voice in the administration of the country.

In the alternative, out of the existing province of the Punjab a new Province may be carved out as an additional provincial unit in the united India of the future in such a way that all the important Sikh *Gurdwaras* and shrines may be included in it as also a substantial majority of the Sikh population in the existing Province of the Punjab.

Memorandum by Akali Dal, leader Master Tara Singh, May 1946, in [11], p. 625.

DOCUMENT 35 JINNAH'S VISION OF A SECULAR PAKISTAN, 1947

... if we want to make this great State of Pakistan happy and prosperous we should wholly and solely concentrate on the well-being of the people and especially, of the masses and the poor. If you will work in co-operation, forgetting the past, burying the hatchet, you are bound to succeed. If you change your past and work together in a spirit that everyone of you, no matter to what community he belongs, no matter what relations he had with you in the past, no matter what is his colour, caste or creed, is first, second and last a citizen of this State with equal rights, privilege and obligations, there will be no end to the progress you will make.

I cannot emphasise it too much. We should begin to work in that spirit and in course of time all these angularities of the majority and minority communities, the Hindu community and the Muslim community – because even as regards Muslims you have Pathans Pujabis, Shias, Sunnis and so on, and among the Hindus you have Brahmans, Vashnavas, Khatris, also Bengalees, Madrasis, and so on – will vanish. Indeed, if you ask me, this has been the biggest hindrance in the way of India to attain freedom and independence and but for this we would have been free peoples long long ago. No power can hold another nation; and specially a nation of 400 million souls in subjection; nobody could have conquered you, and even if it had happened, nobody could have continued its hold on you for any length of time but for this. Therefore, we must learn a lesson from this. You are free; you are free to go to your temples, you are free to go to your mosques or to any other places of worship in this State of Pakistan. You may belong to any religion or caste or creed – that has nothing to do with the business of the State.

Now, I think we should keep that in front of us as our ideal and you will find that in course of time Hindus would cease to be Hindus and Muslims would cease to be Muslims, not in the religious sense, because that is the personal faith of each individual, but in the political sense as citizens of the State. ...

Address to the Constituent Assembly of Pakistan, Karachi, 11 August 1947, in [20], pp. 35–7.

GLOSSARY

ashram   Religious retreat.

babu (*baboo*)   A title of respect, particularly in Bengal; sometimes used disparagingly by the British in India to denote Indians educated in English.

bagh   A garden.

bania   A Hindu from the shopkeeper or merchant caste.

bhadralok   The respectable people in Bengal, mainly (but not exclusively) recruited from the higher, literate Hindu castes.

Brahmins   Hindus belonging to the highest, originally priestly, caste.

dacoity (dacoities)   A robbery committed by *dacoits*; a gang robbery.

darwaza   A gate.

fatwa   An opinion on a point of Islamic law given by a person qualified in that discipline.

gurudwara   A Sikh temple.

howdah   Seating for riders of elephants.

kaffir   One who is ungrateful to God for His gifts, hence an unbeliever to Muslims.

Khalif (Khalifa, Caliph)   A successor to Muhammad as temporal and spiritual head of the Islamic community.

Khilafat   A movement among Indian Muslims in support of the Sultan of Turkey.

kisan   A peasant.

kisan sabhas   Peasant organisations.

Koran   See *Qur'an*.

kshatriya   The warrior caste or status group in Hindu society.

Mahasabha   Literally, 'Great Society'; a Hindu political party.

mofussil   Rural areas as distinct from metropolitan centres.

muhajir (*mohajir*)   Pakistani refugee from India.

mullahs   Hindi corruption of *maula*, meaning learned man, often used in British India for a Muslim schoolmaster.

nawab   Muslim title, comparable to *raja* or *maharaja*; a Muslim nobleman.

pir   A Muslim spiritual guide.

presidency   Presidency was the formal term applied to Bengal, Bombay and Madras, the oldest of the British Indian provinces. The term originated in the seventeenth century when the senior official in each place bore the title of president.

pucca (*pukka*)   Complete; proper; the genuine article.

purdah (*pardah*)   The seclusion of women.

Quaid-i-Azam   Literally, 'Great leader'; title given by Muslims to Muhammad Ali Jinnah.

Qur'an (Koran)   Islamic scripture as revealed to Muhammad.

rayat (*ryot*)   Persian term for a peasant or a cultivator.

sanads   A deed or letter having the force of an edict or ordinance.

sarkar   Mughal imperial administrative unit, sometimes used as a synonym for 'government'.

satyagraha   Literally, 'truth force'; Gandhi's term for non-violent resistance to authority.

satyagrahis   Practitioners of non-violent resistance.

sepoys   Corruption of the Persian word *sipahi*, meaning 'foot soldier'; a soldier in the Indian Army.

shar'ia   Literally, 'the path to be followed'; the divine law of Islam.

Sunni   'One who follows the trodden path', which is to say the model practice of the Prophet and of the early Muslim community; one who does not deviate from the beliefs of the global Muslim community.

swadeshi   The 'Buy Indian' economic strategy of the Indian National Congress.

swaraj   Self-rule.

Tabligh   A Muslim movement for the conversion and reconversion of non-believers.

talukdar (*taluqdar*)   A superior *zamindar* or landlord who engaged with the state for the payment of revenue from his own and other (inferior) estates. After 1858 the British endowed *talukdars* with proprietory rights to conciliate them to British rule.

tamasha   An entertainment; an event.

Tanzim   A Muslim movement for self-defence.

ulema (*ulama*)   Arabic plural of *alim*, a scholar, especially in religious subjects; loosely used to describe the whole Muslim ecclesiastical class.

vakil (*wakil*)   In the nineteenth century, an authorised pleader in a court of justice; more generally, a lawyer.

Vedas   The (four) oldest Hindu scriptures.

Wahabi (Wahhabi)   A puritanical Islamic sect following the doctrines of Abdul-Wahab, an eighteenth-century Arab reformer.

zamindar   A landlord.

WHO'S WHO

Abdul Ghaffar Khan (1890–1988)   Pathan from Peshawar District; entered politics in 1919 during Rowlatt agitation; member of the Congress Working Committee; founded the Khudai Kitmatgar organisation (the 'Redshirts') as a vehicle for Pathan nationalism; played a prominent part in the Civil Disobedience campaigns of the 1930s; strongly opposed the partition of India; after 1947 began agitation for the creation of a separate Pathan state, 'Paktunistan', which led to him being jailed by the Pakistan government.

Aga Khan, Sultan Mahomed Shah (1875–1958)   The third Aga Khan, he was the spiritual chief of the Ismaili sect of the Shia Muslims and president of the Muslim League, 1906–13.

Ambedkar, Dr B.R. (1891–1956)   Gained a PhD in 1916 from Columbia University and began legal practice in Bombay in 1924; by 1928 he had emerged as the leader of the Depressed Classes ('Untouchables'); a member of the governor-general's Executive Council, 1942–46; law minister, 1947–51; on 14 October 1956 he embraced Buddhism and advised his followers to do likewise.

Attlee, Clement (Lord) (1883–1967)   Came into close touch with Indian affairs as a member of the Simon Commission in 1927; leader of the British Labour Party, 1935–55; deputy prime minister, 1942–45; prime minister, 1945–51.

Azad, M.K. (Maulana) (1883–1958)   Received a traditional Islamic education; toured Arab world 1907–9; started the newspaper, *Al-Hilal (The Crescent)*, which soon drew unfavourable notice from the British; joined Congress; became president of the Khilafat Committee in 1920 and of the Nationalist Muslim Conference in 1928; Congress president, 1923 and 1940–46; education minister in the Nehru government, 1947–58.

Banerjea, Surendranath (1848–1925)   Educated Doveton College, Calcutta, he joined the ICS in 1871; dismissed, 1874; professor of English, Metropolitan Institution, 1876; founder and principal, Ripon College, 1882; founder, Indian Association, 1876; proprietor, *Bengalee*, 1878; member of the Bengal Legislative Council, 1893–1901; president of the Indian National Congress, 1895 and 1902.

Baring, Sir Evelyn (Lord Cromer) (1841–1917)   Member of a prominent British merchant banking family; entered the army; served as private secretary to his cousin, Lord Northbrook, during the latter's term as viceroy, 1874–78; comptroller-general, 1879–80; finance member of the viceroy's council, 1880–83; consul-general and minister to Egypt, 1883–1907.

Besant, Mrs Annie (1847–1933)   British theosophist who went to India in 1895; president of the Theosophical Society, 1907–33; founded the Central Hindu College at Banares; established Indian Home Rule League in 1916; interned by the Madras government in 1917; president of Congress, 1917.

Bonnerjee, W.C. (1844–1906)   Barrister of the Calcutta High Court; president of Congress in 1885 and 1892.

Bose, Subhas Chandra (1897–1945)   Educated at Calcutta University; joined the ICS but resigned in 1920; joined Congress; made his mark on national politics in 1928 by demanding complete independence for India; elected Congress president in 1938 and re-elected in 1939, against Gandhi's wishes, but had to resign; founded the Forward Block; in 1941 he escaped house arrest and fled to Germany where he was welcomed by Hitler; went to Japan in 1943 where he set up a provisional government of 'Free India' and took over the command, in October 1943, of the Indian National Army; died in an air crash, 1945.

Chatterjee, Bankim Chandra (1838–94)   A junior official in the Bengal public service; pioneer of Bengali prose literature; his most important novel, *Anandamath,* spawned the poem *Bande Mataram* which became the anthem of the Indian national movement.

Chelmsford, Lord (1868–1933)   Governor of Queensland, 1905–9 and of New South Wales, 1909–13; viceroy of India, 1916–21.

Churchill, (Sir) Winston Spencer (1874–1965)   Conservative MP for Woodford, 1924–64; left Conservative shadow cabinet and opposed concessions to India, in particular the Act of 1935; member of the War Cabinet, 1939–40; British prime minister, 1940–45, 1951–55.

Cripps, Sir Stafford (1889–1952)   Solicitor-general in the British Labour government of 1929–31; Lord Privy Seal and leader of the House of Commons, 1942, in which capacity he visited India in March; also member of the British Cabinet Mission which visited India in March 1946; chancellor of the exchequer, 1947–50.

Curzon, George Nathaniel (Lord) (1859–1925)   Viceroy of India, 1898–1905; British foreign secretary, 1919–24.

Das, C.R. (1870–1925)   Barrister of the Calcutta High Court; entered politics in 1917 and became Congress president in 1921 and 1922; formed, with Motilal Nehru, the Swaraj Party of the Congress in 1923.

Dufferin, Lord (1826–1902)   Governor-general of Canada, 1872–78; viceroy of India, 1884–88.

Dutt, Romesh Chandra (1848–1909). Educated at Presidency College, Calcutta, and University College, London; entered the ICS in 1871; divisional commissioner, 1894; president of Indian National Congress, 1899.

Dyer, Brigadier-General R.E.H. (1864–1927)   Joined the Indian Army in 1888; decorated for services in Burma (1886–87) and on the Northwest Frontier (Hazara, 1888; Waziristan, 1902; Zakka Kehl, 1908), and mentioned in despatches (1914–18 war); commander, Jullundur training brigade, 1917; injured in a riding accident, 1917, suffered increasing paralysis thereafter; responsible for Armritsar Massacre in 1919; appointed to active service in the Afghan War; forced to retire in 1920 after he was censured by an official of the committee of inquiry over his conduct at Amritsar.

Gandhi, Mohandas Karamchand (1869–1948)   Born in Porbandar, Gujarat; studied law in England and was called to the Bar in 1889; did legal and community work in South Africa (1893–1915), where he forged his political weapon of *satyagraha*; the paramount leader of the Indian Nationalist Movement and of Congress from 1920 until his assassination in 1948.

Ghose, Aurobindo (1872–1950)   Gained fame as an extremist and politician from 1906 to 1910, after which he retired to Pondicherry to devote himself to spiritualism.

Gokhale, G.K. (1866–1915)   Poona-based teacher and journalist; founder-member of Congress; member of the Imperial Legislative Council, 1901–15; Congress president, 1905.

Golwalkar, M.S. (1906–73)   Zoology professor at Benaras Hindu University; succeeded K.B. Hedgewar as leader of the Rashtriya Swayamsevak Sangh (RSS), 1940.

Hardinge, Lord (1858–1944)   Joined the British Foreign Office in 1880; permanent under-secretary of state for foreign affairs, 1906; viceroy of India, 1910–16.

Hedgewar, K.B. (1890–1940)   Maharashtrian Brahmin doctor; joined Congress after completing his medical studies in Calcutta; founded the Rashtriya Swayamsevat Sangh (RSS) at Nagpur, 1925.

Hume, A.O. (1829–1912)   Secretary in the Revenue and Agriculture Department, Government of India, 1870–79; retired, 1882; became interested in theosophy; helped found the Indian National Congress in 1885; general secretary of Congress, 1885–1906; author of the standard work on Indian birds.

Iqbal, Sir Mohammad (1876–1938)   Poet and philosopher; president of the All-Indian Muslim League, 1930.

Irwin, Lord (1881–1959)   Viceroy of India, 1926–31; succeeded his father as Viscount Halifax in 1934; British foreign secretary, 1938–40; member of the British War Cabinet, 1939–45.

Jinnah, M.A. (1876–1948)   Born in Karachi; barrister of the Bombay High Court; member of Congress, 1908–20; president of the Muslim League, 1934–48; known to Pakistanis as the Quaid-i-Azam ('Great Leader').

Kipling, Rudyard (1865–1936)   Born in Bombay and raised in Lahore where his father was curator of the museum; after schooling in England, he returned to India to work on the Lahore *Civil and Military Gazette*; won fame with his collection of stories *Plain Tales From the Hills* (1888) but is best known for his novel *Kim* (1901), published after he had returned to England.

Lajpat Rai, Lala (1865–1928)   A lawyer from Punjab; Congress president for the special session held at Calcutta in 1920.

Lawrence, Sir Walter (1857–1940)   Entered the ICS in 1877; served mainly in Punjab and Kashmir; private secretary to the viceroy, Lord Curzon, 1898–1903; chief of staff during the tour of the Prince of Wales, 1905–6; member of secretary of state's Council, 1907–8.

Liaqat Ali Khan (1895–1951)   Barrister from the United Provinces; became general secretary of the Muslim League in 1937; member of the Interim Government, 1946–47; prime minister of Pakistan from August 1947 to 16 October 1951, when he was assassinated.

Linlithgow, Lord (1887–1952)   Deputy chairman of the Conservative and Unionist Party; chairman on the Royal Commission on Agriculture in India, 1926–28; chairman of the Select Committee on Indian Constitutional Reform, 1933–34; viceroy of India, 1936–43.

Lytton, Edward (Lord) (1831–91) Diplomat and writer; viceroy of India, 1876–80.

Macaulay, Thomas Babington (Lord) (1800–59) Educated at Cambridge, made his name as a writer on public affairs before entering parliament in 1830; went to India in 1834 as the first law member of the viceroy's council; returned to England in 1839; served as secretary of war, 1839–41, and paymaster-general, 1846–47; devoted the rest of his life to writing a monumental history of England.

Malaviya, M.M. (1861–1946) UP lawyer; Congress president in 1909 and 1918; member of Imperial Legislative Assembly, 1910–20; helped revive Hindu Mahasabha, 1915; founded Banares Hindu University in 1916.

Mehta, Sir Pherozeshah (1854–1915) Barrister of the Bombay High Court; a liberal politician who kept the extremists out of Congress until his death; Congress president, 1890.

Meston, Sir James S. (1865–1942) Entered the ICS in 1883; secretary, Foreign Department, 1909; lieutenant-governor, United Provinces, 1912; on deputation to the Imperial War Conference and Cabinet, 1917; finance member, Government of India, 1918.

Minto, Lord (1845–1914) Governor-general of Canada, 1898–1904; viceroy of India, 1905–10.

Montagu, Edwin Samuel (1879–1924) Liberal MP, 1906–22; under-secretary for India, 1910–14; secretary of state for India, 1917–22.

Moonje, B.S. (1872–1948) Medical practitioner of Nagpur, Central Provinces; leader of Hindu Mahasabha.

Morley, John (Lord) (1838–1923) Secretary of state in the Liberal government of 1905–10.

Mountbatten, Lord (1900–79) Entered Royal Navy in 1913; supreme allied commander for South-East Asia, 1943–46; viceroy of India, 1947; governor-general of India, August 1947–June 1948.

Muhammad Ali (1878–1931) Educated at Aligarh and Oxford; a pan-Islamist and the prominent leader of the Khilafat movement, for which he was interned twice, 1915–19 and 1921–23; Congress president, 1923.

Naoroji, Dadabhai (1827–1917) Son of a Parsi priest; educated Elphinstone College, Bombay, where he became a professor; started *Rast Goftar*, 1851; active in Bombay Association; founder, East India Association, London, 1866; prime minister, Baroda, 1874; member, Bombay Legislative Council, 1885; MP for Central Finsbury, 1892–95; president of Indian National Congress, 1886, 1893, 1906.

Nehru, Jawaharlal (1889–1964) Educated at Harrow and Cambridge and called to the Bar in 1912; entered politics as a member of the Congress in 1920; Congress president, 1929, 1936, 1937, 1946, 1951–54; vice-president of the Interim Indian Government, 1946–47; prime minister of Independent India, 1947–64.

Nehru, Motilal (1861–1931) Father of Jawaharlal Nehru; advocate of the Allahabad High Court; leader of the Congress Swaraj Party, 1923–26; president of Congress, 1919 and 1928.

O'Dwyer, Sir Michael (1864–1940)   Entered the ICS in 1885; lieutenant-governor of Punjab, 1913–19; shot dead by an Indian terrorist in London.

Orwell, George (pseud.) (1903–50)   Born in India, he returned to serve in the Burma Police, 1922–27; retired from public service to concentrate on writing; his works include *Burmese Days* (1935) and the prophetic *Nineteen Eighty-four* (1940).

Pal, B.C. (1858–1932)   Bengali journalist and author; active in politics as an extremist in the first decade of the twentieth century.

Patel, Vallabhbhai (1875–1950)   Gujarati lawyer; municipal councillor, Ahmedabad; organised Bardoli *satyagraha*, 1928; Congress president, 1930; home member in the Interim Indian Government, 1947; deputy prime minister of India, 1947–50.

Prasad, Rajendra (1884–1963)   Bihari lawyer; Congress president in 1934, 1935, 1939 and 1947; first president of the Indian Republic, 1950–62.

Radcliffe, Sir Cyril (1899–1977)   Fellow of All Souls' College, Oxford, 1922–27; called to the Bar, 1924; director-general, British Ministry of Information, 1941–45; chairman of the Indian Boundary Commission, 1947; chairman of Trustees British Museum, 1963–68; chancellor of Warwick University, 1966–77.

Rajagopalachari, C.R. (1879–1972)   Lawyer from Madras; chief minister of Madras, 1937–39 and 1952–54; governor-general of India, 1948–50; founder-leader of the Swatantra Party, 1959.

Ranade, Mahadev Govind (1841–1901)   Chitpavan Brahmin; one of the first graduates of Bombay University; Professor of English, Elphinstone College, 1868–71; judge, High Court of Bombay, 1893; member of Bombay Legislative Council.

Ripon, Lord (1827–1909)   Liberal politician; viceroy of India, 1880–84.

Saiyyid Ahmed Khan (1817–98)   Born in Delhi; entered the service of the English East India Company, 1837; rose to the rank of subordinate judge; founded Aligarh Scientific Society and the Muhammadan Anglo-Oriental College, 1875; additional member, governor-general's Legislative Council, 1878–83.

Salisbury, Robert (Lord) (1830–1903)   British Conservative politician; as Viscount Cranbourne served as secretary of state for India, 1866–67 and 1874–78; British foreign secretary 1878–80, 1885–86, 1886–92 and 1895–1900; prime minister, 1885–86, 1886–92 and 1895–1902.

Savarkar, V.D. (1883–1966)   Extremist Maharashtrian Brahmin politician, captured and jailed in the Andaman Islands for terrorist activities in 1910; joined the Hindu Mahasabha in 1924 and was its president, 1938–42.

Sen, Keshub Chandra (1838–1884)   Educated at Presidency College, Calcutta; a staunch loyalist who became an ardent religious reformer; reorganised Brahmo Samaj (Society of God), 1875–78.

Simon, Sir John (1873–1954)   British attorney-general, 1913–15; chairman of the 'Simon Commission' 1927–30; British foreign secretary, 1931–35.

Sinha, Lord (Sir Satyendra) (1864–1928) Advocate-general, Bengal, 1916; member of the Bengal legislature, 1916–19; on deputation to the Imperial War Conference and Cabinet, 1917 and 1918; parliamentary under-secretary of state, 1919–20; governor of Bihar and Orissa, 1921.

Strachey, Sir John (1823–1907) Educated at Haileybury in preparation for a career in the ICS; served in NWFP and Central Provinces where he rose to the rank of chief judge; president, Sanitary Commission, 1864; chief commissioner of Oudh, 1866; additional member of the Viceroy's council, 1868–74; lieutenant-governor, NWFP, 1876; finance member, Viceroy's council, 1876–80; member of the secretary of state's council, 1885–95.

Suhrawardy, H.S (1892–1963) Educated in Calcutta and Britain; called to the Bar; member, Bengal Legislative Council, 1921–36, during which time he also served as deputy mayor of Calcutta and secretary, Bengal Provincial Muslim League; minister in the Government of Bengal, 1937–41 and 1943–45; chief minister of Bengal, 1943–45; moved to East Pakistan in 1949; founded Awami Muslim League; prime minister of Pakistan 1956–57.

Tagore, Sir Rabindranath (1861–1941) Member of a prominent Bengali *bhadralok* family; prolific and gifted writer, dramatist and painter; first Asian to win the Nobel Prize for Literature (1916); rejected extreme nationalism, but returned his knighthood in protest at the Amritsar Massacre of 1919.

Tilak, B.G. (1856–1920) Journalist and author; became leader of extremist wing of Congress; imprisoned for seditious speeches and for articles in his newspapers, *Kesari* and *Mahratta* from 1908 to 1914; founded Home Rule League, 1916.

Tyabji, Badruddin (1844–1906) Bohra Muslim; educated in England; became leading Bombay barrister; member, Bombay Municipal Corporation, 1873–83 and Bombay Legislative Council, 1882–86; founded Anjuman–i-Islam of Bombay, 1876; founder member, Bombay Presidency Association, 1885; president, 1887; judge of the High Court of Bombay, 1895.

Vivekananda, Swami (Narendranath Datta) (1863–1902) Charismatic Calcutta-born Hindu social reformer and missionary; gained international fame after speaking at the World Parliament of Religions at Chicago, 1893.

Wacha, Sir Dinshaw Edulji (1844–1936) Parsi; mill owner in Bombay; Congress President, 1901.

Wavell, Archibald Percival (Lord) (1883–1950) Commander-in-chief, Middle East, 1939–41; of India, 1941–43; supreme commander, South West Pacific, 1942; viceroy of India, 1943–47.

BIBLIOGRAPHY

Unless otherwise stated, place of publication is London.

OFFICIAL REPORTS

1   Datta, K.L. (Chairman), *Official Report on the Enquiry into the Rise of Prices in India*, Superintendent of Government Printing, Calcutta, 1914
2   Joint Select Committee on Constitutional Reform [Session 1933–34], *Report*, Vol. 1, Part 1, HMSO, 1934
3   *Report of the Disorders Inquiry Committee, 1919–20*, repr., Deep Publications, Delhi, 1976
4   *Report of the Public Service Commission, 1886–87*, Superintendent of Government Printing, Calcutta, 1888
5   *Report on Indian Constitutional Reform*, Superintendent of Government Printing, Calcutta, 1918

COLLECTIONS OF DOCUMENTS

6   Bennett, George (ed.), *The Concept of Empire: Burke to Attlee 1774–1947*, 2nd edn, Adam and Charles Black, 1967
7   Bombay, Government of (comp.), *Sources for a History of the Freedom Movement in India*, Government Central Press, Bombay, 1958, Vol. II
8   Chopra, P.N. (ed.), *Quit India Movement: British Secret Documents*, Interprint, New Delhi, 1986
9   Chopra, P.N. and Jha, Padmsha (eds), *Secret Papers from the British Royal Archives*, Konark Publishers Private Ltd, Delhi, 1998
10 de Bary, W.T. et. al. (eds), *Sources of Indian Tradition*, Columbia University Press, New York, 1958
11 Gwyer, Sir Maurice and Appadorai, A. (eds), *Speeches and Documents on the Indian Constitution 1921–47*, Vol. II, Oxford University Press, Bombay, 1957
12 Hasan, Mushirul (ed.), *India Partitioned: The Other Face of Freedom*, Vol. II, Roli Books, New Delhi, 1995
13 Iyer, Raghavan (ed.), *The Essential Writings of Mahatma Gandhi*, Oxford University Press, Delhi, 1996
14 Mansergh, N. and Lumby, E.W.R. (eds), *The Transfer of Power 1942–7*, Vol. 1, HMSO, 1970
15 McLane, J.R. (ed.), *The Political Awakening in India*, Prentice-Hall Inc., Englewood Cliffs, NJ, 1970
16 Moore, Clark D. and Eldredge, David (eds), *India Yesterday and Today*, Bantam Pathfinder Editions, Toronto, 1970

17   Norman, Dorothy (ed.), *Nehru: the First Sixty Years*, 2 vols, Bodley Head, 1965

18   Pandey, B.N. (ed.), *The Indian Nationalist Movement, 1885–1947: Select Documents*, Macmillan, 1979

19   Philips, C.H. (ed.), *The Evolution of India and Pakistan: Select Documents*, Oxford University Press, 1962

20   *Quaid-i-Azam Speaks: His Vision of Pakistan*, Quaid-i-Azam Academy, Karachi, 1991

21   *The Collected Works of Mahatma Gandhi*, Publications Division, Ministry of Information and Broadcasting, Government of India, Delhi, Vol. XVIII, 1965

MEMOIRS, DIARIES AND CONTEMPORARY ACCOUNTS

22   Balfour, Lady Betty (ed.), *Personal and Literary Letters of Robert First Earl of Lytton*, Vol. 2, Longmans, Green and Co., 1906

23   Banerjea, Sir Surendranath, *A Nation in Making*, repr., Oxford University Press, Bombay, 1963

24   Besant, Annie, *India Bond or Free? A World Problem*, G.P. Putnam's Sons Ltd, 1926

25   Chaudhuri, Nirad C., *The Autobiography of an Unknown Indian*, The Hogarth Press, 1987 [1st published 1951]

26   Chirol, Valentine, *Indian Unrest*, Macmillan and Co. Ltd., 1910

27   Dutt, Romesh, *The Economic History of India in the Victorian Age*, Kegan Paul, Trench, Trubner and Co. Ltd., 1903

28   Gilbert, Martin (ed.), *Servant of India: a Study of Imperial Rule from 1905 to 1910 as Told through the Correspondence and Diaries of Sir James Dunlop Smith*, Longmans, 1966

29   Hazari, Rabindra K., *Untouchable*, Frederick A. Praeger, Inc., New York, 1969

30   Moon, Sir Penderel (ed.), *Wavell: the Viceroy's Journal*, Oxford University Press, 1973

31   Nehru, Jawaharlal, *An Autobiography, With Musings on Recent Events in India*, Allied Publishers Private Ltd, Bombay, 1962 [1st published 1936]

32   O'Dwyer, Sir Michael, *India As I Knew It 1885–1925*, Constable and Company, 1925

33   Strachey, John, *India: its Administration and Progress*, 4th, rev. edn, Macmillan, 1911

34   Tandon, Prakash, *Punjabi Century 1857–1947*, California University Press, Berkeley, CA, 1961

35   *The Collected Essays, Journalism and Letters of George Orwell*, Vol. 1 (eds Sonia Orwell and Ian Angus), Secker and Warburg, 1968

OTHER BOOKS

36   Anderson, Benedict, *Imagined Communities: Reflections on the Origin and Spread of Nationalism*, Verso, 1992

37   Bose, Sugata and Jalal, Ayesha, *Modern South Asia: History, Culture, Political Economy*, Oxford University Press, Delhi, 1999

38   Brown, Judith M., *Modern India: the Origins of an Asian Democracy*, Oxford University Press, Delhi, 1985

39   Chandra, Bipan, et. al., *India's Struggle for Independence 1857–1947*, Penguin Books, (India) Ltd, New Delhi, 1989

40   Copland, Ian, *The Princes of India in the End-Game of Empire, 1917–1947*, Cambridge University Press, Cambridge, 1997

41   Coupland, R., *The Indian Problem 1833–1935* Oxford University Press, 1942

42   French, Patrick, *Liberty or Death: India's Journey to Independence and Division*, Harper-Collins, 1998

43   Gopal, S., *British Policy in India 1858–1905*, Cambridge University Press, Cambridge 1965

44   Griffiths, Sir Percival, *The British Impact on India*, Frank Cass and Company Ltd., 1965

45   Guha, Ranajit, *Dominance without Hegemony: History and Power in Colonial India*, Harvard University Press, Cambridge, MA, 1997

46   Hutchins, Francis G., *The Illusion of Permanence: British Imperialism in India*, Princeton University Press, Princeton, NJ; 1967

47   Inden, Ronald, *Imagining India*, Basil Blackwell, Oxford, 1990

48   Jalal, Ayesha, *The Sole Spokesman: Jinnah, the Muslim League and the Demand for Pakistan*, Cambridge University Press, Cambridge, 1985

49   Low, D.A. (ed.), *Congress and the Raj: Facets of the Indian Struggle 1917–47*, Arnold-Heinemann, 1977

50   Low, D.A., *Eclipse of Empire*, Cambridge University Press, Cambridge 1991

51   Mansergh, Nicholas, *The Commonwealth Experience*, Weidenfeld and Nicholson Ltd, 1969

52   Masselos, Jim, *Indian Nationalism: a History*, Sterling Publishers Private Ltd, New Delhi, 1985

53   McCully, Bruce Tiebout, *English Education and the Origins of Indian Nationalism*, Peter Smith, Gloucester, MA, 1966

54   McLane, John R., *Indian Nationalism and the Early Congress*, Princeton University Press, Princeton, NJ, 1977

55   Metcalf, Thomas R., *Ideologies of the Raj (New Cambridge History of India, III.4)*, Cambridge University Press, Cambridge 1994

56   Metcalf, Thomas R., *Land, Landlords and the British Raj: Northern India in the Nineteenth Century*, California University Press, Berkeley, CA, 1979

57   Pandey, B.N., *The Breakup of British India*, Macmillan, 1969

58   Reeves, Peter, *Landlords and Governments in Uttar Pradesh: a Study of Their Relations until Zamindari Abolition*, Oxford University Press, Bombay, 1991

59   Robb, P.G., *The Government of India and Reform: Policies towards Politics and the Constitution, 1916–1921*, Oxford University Press, 1976

60   Sarkar, Sumit, *Modern India 1885–1947*, Macmillan India Ltd, Madras, 1983

61   Seal, Anil, *The Emergence of Indian Nationalism: Competition and Collaboration in the Later Nineteenth Century*, Cambridge University Press, 1968

62   Sinha, Mrinalini, *Colonial Masculinity: the 'Manly Englishman' and the 'Effeminate Bengali' in the Late Nineteenth Century*, Kali For Women, New Delhi, 1995

63   Spangenberg, Bradford, *British Bureaucracy in India: Status, Policy and the ICS in the Late Nineteenth Century*, Manohar, New Delhi, 1976
64   Stein, Burton, *A History of India*, Blackwell Publishers, Oxford, 1998
65   Stokes, Eric, *The Peasant and the Raj: Studies in Agrarian Society and Peasant Rebellion in Colonial India*, Vikas Publishing House Private Ltd, New Delhi, 1978
66   Washbrook, D.A., *The Emergence of Provincial Politics: the Madras Presidency, 1870–1920*, Cambridge University Press, Cambridge 1976
67   Whitcombe, Elizabeth, *Agrarian Conditions in Northern India,* Vol. I: *the United Provinces under British Rule 1860–1900*, California University Press, Berkeley, CA,1972
68   Wolpert, Stanley, *A New History of India*, 5th edn, Oxford University Press, New York, 1997
69   Wolpert, Stanley, *Morley and India 1906–1910*, California University Press, Berkeley, CA, 1967
70   Woodruff, Philip (pseud.), *The Men Who Ruled India,* Vol. 2: *The Guardians*, Jonathan Cape, 1965
71   Wurgaft, Lewis D., *The Imperial Imagination: Magic and Myth in Kipling's India*, Wesleyan University Press, Middletown, CT, 1983

ARTICLES

72   Amin, Shahid, 'Gandhi as Mahatma: Gorakhpur District, Eastern UP, 1921–2', in Ranajit Guha (ed.), *Subaltern Studies III: Writings on South Asian History and Society*, Oxford University Press, Delhi, 1984
73   Brasted, H.V. and Bridge, Carl, 'The Historiography of Power in South Asia: an Historiographical Review', *South Asia*, n.s., XVII, 1994
74   Danzig, Richard, 'The Announcement of August 20th, 1917', *Journal of Asian Studies*, 28, 1967
75   Gallagher, John, 'The Decline, Revival and Fall of the British Empire', in Anil Seal (ed.), *The Decline, Revival and Fall of the British Empire: the Ford Lectures and Other Essays*, Cambridge University Press, Cambridge, 1982
76   Gilmartin, David, '"Divine Displeasure" and Muslim Elections: the Shaping of Community in Twentieth Century Punjab', in D.A. Low (ed.), *The Political Inheritance of Pakistan*, Macmillan, 1991
77   Krishna, Gopal, 'The Development of the Indian National Congress as a Mass Organization, 1918–23', *Journal of Asian Studies*, 25, 1965–66
78   Potter, David, 'Manpower Shortage and the End of Colonialism: the Case of the Indian Civil Service', *Modern Asian Studies*, 7, 1973
79   Tomlinson, B.R., 'India and the British Empire, 1880–1935', *The Indian Economic and Social History Review*, XII, 1972

INDEX

Aga Khan, the, 55, 120
Ahmad Khan, Sir Saiyyid, 9, 53–4, 61, 106, 124
    antagonism towards the Congress, 105
Ahmedabad, xvii, 48, 52
Akali Dal, *see* Shiromani Akali Dal
Ali, Amir, 54
Ali, Chaudhri Rahmat, 61
Ali, Muhammad, xvi, 11, 123
Ali Khan, Liaquat, 60, 77, 122
Aligarh, 9–10, 54, 58, 63
All-India Muslim League, xvi, xviii, 55–6, 59–60, 70–4, 83–4, 86, 108–9, 113–14, 116
All-India Spinners' Association, 51
Ambedkar, Bhim Rao, xvii, 51, 120
Ampthill, Lord, 34
Amritsar, 5, 23, 79, 94–5
Andaman Islands, 5
Archbold, W.A.J., 106
Arya Samaj, 41, 43, 56, 58–9
Attlee, Clement (Lord Attlee), 70, 75, 120
Awadh, *see* Oudh
Azad, Maulana A.K., 74, 120

Balfour Declaration (1926), 29
Banerjea, Sir Surendranath, 34–7, 41, 44–5, 120
Bangladesh, 76
Baring, Sir Evelyn, 26, 30, 120
Bengal, 36, 53, 55, 63, 65, 71, 73–4, 77, 106
    bhadralok of, 8, 26, 34–5, 54, 118
    partition of, xvi, 11, 27, 44
    revolutionary violence in, 22–3, 67, 91, 110
Besant, Annie, 45–6, 120
Bikaner, Maharaja of, 9
Bombay, 22, 25, 28, 33, 36–7, 75
Bonnerjee, W.C., 120
Bose, Rash Behari, 44
Bose, Subhas Chandra, xvii, xviii, 35, 51, 65, 121
Britain, legacy in India, 75–6, 78

Cabinet Mission (1946), xviii, 72–4, 113–14
Calcutta, xviii, 8, 36, 44, 54, 65, 73, 77
    University of, 10
Cambridge School, 85
Canning, Lord, 8
Chamber of Princes, 9

Champaran Satyagraha, 47
Chapekar, Damodar, 33–4, 98–9
Chatterji, Bankim Chandra, 17, 43, 121
Chauri Chaura incident (1922), 49, 103,
Chelmsford, Lord, 25, 28, 101–2, 121
Chetwode, Sir Phillip, 30, 97
Chitpavan Brahmins, 20, 22, 42, 66
Churchill, Sir Winston, 22, 69, 111–12, 121
Civil Disobedience Movement (1930–34), xvii, 52, 67
Civil Disobedience Movement (1940–41), 67
Communal Award (1932), xvii
Communal (Hindu–Muslim) riots, xviii, 57–8, 73–4, 77, 106–7, 114–16
Communist Party of India, xvi, xvii, 66, 76
Congress Party, *see* Indian National Congress
Cow protection movement, 107
Cripps Sir Stafford, 66, 70, 121
    mission to India (1942), xviii, 69, 71, 112–13
Curzon, George Nathaniel, 3, 11, 17, 26–7, 29, 44, 84, 121
    attitude to the Congress, 93

Dacca, Syed Nawab Ali Chowdry of, 55, 106
Das, Chittaranjan, 59, 121
Delhi, xvi, 23, 63, 77
    'Assemblage' (1877), 8
    Durbar (1903), 8
Deoband Seminary, 56
Dhar, Pandit Bishan Narayan, 58
Digby, William, 32–3
Direct Action Day (1946), 73
Dominion Status, xviii, 29, 51, 104–5
Dufferin, Lord, ix, 11, 24, 121
Dutt, Romesh Chandra, 32–3, 97, 121
Dyer, Brigadier-General Reginald, 5, 23, 48, 94–5, 121

English East India Company, 10, 33
Europeans in India, 3, 5, 18
    racism among, 34, 93–4

Fuller, Sir Bampflyde, 55

Gandhi, Indira, 76
Gandhi, Mohandas Karamchand, xvi, xvii, 7, 40, 45, 67, 75, 77, 101–2, 110, 121
    leads Non-Cooperation Movement, 49–51, 102–3
    philosophy of, 46–7, 101

SEMINAR STUDIES IN HISTORY

General Editors: Clive Emsley & Gordon Martel

The series was founded by Patrick Richardson in 1966. Between 1980 and 1996 Roger Lockyer edited the series before handing over to Clive Emsley (Professor of History at the Open University) and Gordon Martel (Professor of International History at the University of Northern British Columbia, Canada and Senior Research Fellow at De Montfort University).

MEDIEVAL ENGLAND

The Pre-Reformation Church in England 1400–1530 (Second edition)
Christopher Harper-Bill   0 582 28989 0

Lancastrians and Yorkists: The Wars of the Roses
David R Cook   0 582 35384 X

TUDOR ENGLAND

Henry VII (Third edition)
Roger Lockyer & Andrew Thrush   0 582 20912 9

Henry VIII (Second edition)
M D Palmer   0 582 35437 4

Tudor Rebellions (Fourth edition)
Anthony Fletcher & Diarmaid MacCulloch   0 582 28990 4

The Reign of Mary I (Second edition)
Robert Tittler   0 582 06107 5

Early Tudor Parliaments 1485–1558
Michael A R Graves   0 582 03497 3

The English Reformation 1530–1570
W J Sheils   0 582 35398 X

Elizabethan Parliaments 1559–1601 (Second edition)
Michael A R Graves   0 582 29196 8

England and Europe 1485–1603 (Second edition)
Susan Doran   0 582 28991 2

The Church of England 1570–1640
Andrew Foster   0 582 35574 5

STUART BRITAIN

Social Change and Continuity: England 1550–1750 (Second edition)
Barry Coward   0 582 29442 8

James I (Second edition)
S J Houston   0 582 20911 0

The English Civil War 1640–1649
Martyn Bennett   0 582 35392 0

Charles I, 1625–1640
Brian Quintrell   0 582 00354 7

The English Republic 1649–1660 (Second edition)
Toby Barnard   0 582 08003 7

Radical Puritans in England 1550–1660
R J Acheson   0 582 35515 X

The Restoration and the England of Charles II (Second edition)
John Miller   0 582 29223 9

The Glorious Revolution (Second edition)
John Miller   0 582 29222 0

EARLY MODERN EUROPE

The Renaissance (Second edition)
Alison Brown   0 582 30781 3

The Emperor Charles V
Martyn Rady   0 582 35475 7

French Renaissance Monarchy: Francis I and Henry II (Second edition)
Robert Knecht   0 582 28707 3

The Protestant Reformation in Europe
Andrew Johnston   0 582 07020 1

The French Wars of Religion 1559–1598 (Second edition)
Robert Knecht   0 582 28533 X

Phillip II
Geoffrey Woodward   0 582 07232 8

The Thirty Years' War
Peter Limm   0 582 35373 4

Louis XIV
Peter Campbell   0 582 01770 X

Spain in the Seventeenth Century
Graham Darby   0 582 07234 4

Peter the Great
William Marshall   0 582 00355 5

EUROPE 1789-1918

Britain and the French Revolution
Clive Emsley   0 582 36961 4

Revolution and Terror in France 1789–1795 (Second edition)
D G Wright   0 582 00379 2

Napoleon and Europe
D G Wright   0 582 35457 9

Nineteenth-Century Russia: Opposition to Autocracy
Derek Offord   0 582 35767 5

The Constitutional Monarchy in France 1814–48
Pamela Pilbeam   0 582 31210 8

The 1848 Revolutions (Second edition)
Peter Jones   0 582 06106 7

The Italian Risorgimento
M Clark   0 582 00353 9

Bismark & Germany 1862–1890 (Second edition)
D G Williamson   0 582 29321 9

Imperial Germany 1890–1918
Ian Porter, Ian Armour and Roger Lockyer   0 582 03496 5

The Dissolution of the Austro-Hungarian Empire 1867–1918 (Second edition)
John W Mason   0 582 29466 5

Second Empire and Commune: France 1848–1871 (Second edition)
William H C Smith   0 582 28705 7

France 1870–1914 (Second edition)
Robert Gildea   0 582 29221 2

The Scramble for Africa (Second edition)
M E Chamberlain   0 582 36881 2

Late Imperial Russia 1890–1917
John F Hutchinson   0 582 32721 0

The First World War
Stuart Robson   0 582 31556 5

EUROPE SINCE 1918

The Russian Revolution (Second edition)
Anthony Wood   0 582 35559 1

Lenin's Revolution: Russia, 1917–1921
David Marples   0 582 31917 X

Stalin and Stalinism (Second edition)
Martin McCauley   0 582 27658 6

The Weimar Republic (Second edition)
John Hiden   0 582 28706 5

The Inter-War Crisis 1919–1939
Richard Overy   0 582 35379 3

Fascism and the Right in Europe, 1919–1945
Martin Blinkhorn   0 582 07021 X

Spain's Civil War (Second edition)
Harry Browne   0 582 28988 2

The Third Reich (Second edition)
D G Williamson   0 582 20914 5

The Origins of the Second World War (Second edition)
R J Overy   0 582 29085 6

The Second World War in Europe
Paul MacKenzie   0 582 32692 3

Anti-Semitism before the Holocaust
Albert S Lindemann   0 582 36964 9

The Holocaust: The Third Reich and the Jews
David Engel   0 582 32720 2

Germany from Defeat to Partition, 1945–1963
D G Williamson   0 582 29218 2

Britain and Europe since 1945
Alex May   0 582 30778 3

Eastern Europe 1945–1969: From Stalinism to Stagnation
Ben Fowkes   0 582 32693 1

Eastern Europe since 1970
Bülent Gökay   0 582 32858 6

The Khrushchev Era, 1953–1964
Martin McCauley   0 582 27776 0

NINETEENTH-CENTURY BRITAIN

Britain before the Reform Acts: Politics and Society 1815–1832
Eric J Evans   0 582 00265 6

Parliamentary Reform in Britain c. 1770–1918
Eric J Evans   0 582 29467 3

Democracy and Reform 1815–1885
D G Wright   0 582 31400 3

Poverty and Poor Law Reform in Nineteenth-Century Britain, 1834–1914:
From Chadwick to Booth
David Englander   0 582 31554 9

The Birth of Industrial Britain: Economic Change, 1750–1850
Kenneth Morgan   0 582 29833 4

Chartism (Third edition)
Edward Royle   0 582 29080 5

Peel and the Conservative Party 1830–1850
Paul Adelman   0 582 35557 5

Gladstone, Disraeli and later Victorian Politics (Third edition)
Paul Adelman   0 582 29322 7

Britain and Ireland: From Home Rule to Independence
Jeremy Smith   0 582 30193 9

TWENTIETH-CENTURY BRITAIN

The Rise of the Labour Party 1880–1945 (Third edition)
Paul Adelman   0 582 29210 7

The Conservative Party and British Politics 1902–1951
Stuart Ball   0 582 08002 9

The Decline of the Liberal Party 1910–1931 (Second edition)
Paul Adelman   0 582 27733 7

The British Women's Suffrage Campaign 1866–1928
Harold L Smith   0 582 29811 3

War & Society in Britain 1899–1948
Rex Pope   0 582 03531 7

The British Economy since 1914: A Study in Decline?
Rex Pope   0 582 30194 7

Unemployment in Britain between the Wars
Stephen Constantine   0 582 35232 0

The Attlee Governments 1945–1951
Kevin Jefferys   0 582 06105 9

The Conservative Governments 1951–1964
Andrew Boxer   0 582 20913 7

Britain under Thatcher
Anthony Seldon and Daniel Collings   0 582 31714 2

INTERNATIONAL HISTORY

The Eastern Question 1774–1923 (Second edition)
A L Macfie   0 582 29195 X

India 1885–1947: The Unmaking of an Empire
Ian Copland   0 582 38173 8

The Origins of the First World War (Second edition)
Gordon Martel   0 582 28697 2

The United States and the First World War
Jennifer D Keene   0 582 35620 2

Anti-Semitism before the Holocaust
Albert S Lindemann   0 582 36964 9

The Origins of the Cold War, 1941–1949 (Second edition)
Martin McCauley   0 582 27659 4

Russia, America and the Cold War, 1949–1991
Martin McCauley   0 582 27936 4

The Arab–Israeli Conflict
Kirsten E Schulze   0 582 31646 4

The United Nations since 1945: Peacekeeping and the Cold War
Norrie MacQueen   0 582 35673 3

Decolonisation: The British Experience since 1945
Nicholas J White   0 582 29087 2

The Origins of the Vietnam War
Fredrik Logevall   0 582 31918 8

The Vietnam War
Mitchell Hall   0 582 32859 4

WORLD HISTORY

China in Transformation 1900–1949
Colin Mackerras   0 582 31209 4

Japan faces the World, 1925–1952
Mary L Hanneman   0 582 36898 7

Japan in Transformation, 1952–2000
Jeff Kingston   0 582 41875 5

US HISTORY

American Abolitionists
Stanley Harrold   0 582 35738 1

The American Civil War, 1861–1865
Reid Mitchell   0 582 31973 0

America in the Progressive Era, 1890–1914
Lewis L Gould   0 582 35671 7

The United States and the First World War
Jennifer D Keene   0 582 35620 2

The Truman Years, 1945–1953
Mark S Byrnes   0 582 32904 3

The Korean War
Steven Hugh Lee   0 582 31988 9

The Origins of the Vietnam War
Fredrik Logevall   0 582 31918 8

The Vietnam War
Mitchell Hall   0 582 32859 4